'Shay Healy is a wonderfully warm and engaging storyteller. He details the events of his life with an hilarious and sometimes rueful bemusement. A huge enjoyment ... will have the reader calling for more.'

Gabriel Byrne

SHAY HEALY has had a long and varied career as a performer, songwriter, television presenter/producer, journalist, documentary film-maker and record producer as well as being the author of a number of books. He lives in Dublin.

ON THE ROAD

SHAY HEALY

THE O'BRIEN PRESS
DUBLIN

First published 2005 by The O'Brien Press Ltd,
20 Victoria Road, Dublin 6, Ireland.
Tel: +353 1 4923333; Fax: +353 1 4922777
E-mail: books@obrien.ie
Website: www.obrien.ie

ISBN: 0-86278-949-4

British Library Cataloguing-in-Publication Data
Healy, Shay
On the road
1.Healy, Shay 2.Television personalities - Ireland - Biography
3.Lyricists - Ireland - Biography 4.Novelists, English - Ireland - Biography
I.Title
791.4'5'028'092

1 2 3 4 5 6 7 8 9 10
05 06 07 08 09 10

Editing, typesetting, layout and design: The O'Brien Press Ltd
Printing: Cox & Wyman Ltd

DEDICATION

This book is dedicated to all the musicians that have
brightened my life with their talent and their company.
And to my family for holding me up when every fibre of my
being was screaming to lie down.

CONTENTS

INTRODUCTION

The country singer, Tom T Hall, once said to me in an interview: 'A book is a supreme vanity,' and that's something I have never forgotten. So in writing down this account of some of the adventures in my life I have tried to avoid vanity, hubris, smugness and self-satisfaction and to just be a simple, honest storyteller.

Life has a habit of twisting the joke when you least expect it, and in a lot of the stories I am the butt of my own jokes. That suits me fine. A sense of humour has been my ally in the good times and my consolation in the bad.

Enjoy … I did.

Chapter 1

U2 CAN HAVE A BUDDY
LIKE MINE

Bono sidles up to me and gives me a great, big smile. Just hours before, he has been married to his beloved Ali, but at this moment that is not the reason for his smile. He is smiling now because he knows how easily the evening might have got away from him – if the wrong person had been allowed choose the band. The wrong kind of band can ruin a good night, but this band is doing everything right. Whoever has booked this band has pulled off the equivalent of an A & R coup.

A & R stands for artist & repertoire. A & R men and women are the people who decide who gets signed to a record label and who doesn't. They are supposed to know about music, but most A & R people are assholes with cloth ears, who know little about anything. Invariably they are loud vulgarians who have a natural talent for abusing their position. Their biggest fears in life come to them as a pair. Firstly, they are petrified that someone else will sign a hit act before them. And secondly, they are knee-knockingly terrified that their bosses will find out that they have no idea what a hit act should sound like.

The most famous A & R decision in history was made by a man called Dick Rowe, who was working at Decca Records in the early Sixties. A thrusting young Jewish manager came to him with the tapes of a four-piece band who wrote most of their own songs. Dick Rowe listened politely, but he just couldn't hear it. And so it came to pass that Dick Rowe told this young manager to be on his way and not to forget to take his band with the stupid name with him. And as we all know since, Brian Epstein was a very good manager. As for the band with the stupid name, The Beatles, they didn't do too badly either.

As young Bono squeezes my arm, I am choking back the urge to tell him that he is a man of great charity and understanding, a man who is able to turn the other cheek and forget about the past, a man who can forgive insult without rancour, a man who chooses not to remind me that I am the Dick Rowe of Irish pundits: the man who said of the emerging U2 on national television, 'I can't really relate to U2 on an honest level. I don't particularly like that kind of music. It doesn't do anything for me.'

And now, despite the awful things I said about him, here I am standing beside Bono at his wedding party, listening to his wedding band, The Cyclones, playing a blinder. In his eyes I see Bono's gratitude for the man who picked such a brilliant wedding band. I nod in acknowledgement of the smile. The man who booked the wedding band is ME.

How or why Bono chose me for the task, I no longer remember. It's not like we were bosom buddies or anything. He probably just thought of me as a brilliant man of music. Ho hum. Anyway, I responded immediately because I knew I had just the band for the occasion. The lead singer, Brian Whelan, and the bass player, Don Byrne, had been my classmates at Westland Row Christian Brothers' school for twelve years. And I had danced many times to the sound of The Cyclones in tennis clubs all over the southside of Dublin.

Now, mentioning the southside reminds me that there was one piece of information I had not disclosed to the U2 office when I booked the wedding band, for fear it might have queered the pitch: The Cyclones were a southside band! In Dublin, the River Liffey neatly bisects the city into northside and southside. These two sides are as polarised as any of the other great cultural divides in the world. But any southsider can tell you that people on the southside are cool and groovy, and people on the northside are skangers. I live on the southside.

And in case you didn't know ... horror of horrors ... let it be whispered ... on 21 August 1982, Bono and Ali – the coolest couple on the planet – got married on the northside!

We gather for the 'afters' party in Sutton House Hotel on the coast road. Prophetically, to cheers from the crowd, Bono is carried like a young Messiah into the room on the shoulders of his brothers and friends. A rock 'n' roll frenzy begins when Irish rock star, Paul Brady, joins the band on stage. Barry Devlin, bass player with Horslips, is next to join in. And that's when Bono and The Edge decide to get in on the act as well. Now we have a real party going and my reputation has been restored to me in no uncertain fashion.

Despite my redemption, it takes another eighteen years before I get any other kind of invitation from U2. But when the offer comes, I am not afraid to be selfish enough to desert my best friend in America so that I can hob-nob with the band.

I am in Nashville, writing a few songs, and U2 are playing in Birmingham, Alabama, which is just four hours away. A couple of phone calls is all it takes to organise backstage passes for myself and my bass player and best friend in America, Jake Mayer. We are soon barreling down Interstate 65 with the radio turned up loud. Memories of previous journeys I had shared with Jake come flooding back.

Jake is from a smallish town in Kentucky, called Owensboro. When we used to gig together, I had a little routine where I would introduce Jake as being from the exotically named Possum Trot, Kentucky. He would contradict me and announce that he was from Owensboro. That was my cue to break into song:

Owensboro
Life is not much fun
Owensboro,
'Cept you sit out in the sun
Owensboro
You might as well be dead

'Cos there ain't no fun in Owensboro
'Less your neck is red.

Jake is the most unfussed person I have ever met. He is small but has a chest that sticks out proudly in front and his voice is low, like a bullfrog. He is very smart and very erudite, but even so, he uses the most improbable folksy Americanisms. For instance, if he gets frustrated, he actually says, 'Dadgummit,' a word that belongs only in newspaper cartoons. And when he writes something down for me on paper, he says, 'I hope y'all can read my chicken scratchins'.

The only time I ever heard Jake get really excited was during a trip from Nashville to Chattanooga. I'm driving. Suddenly, Jake shouts, 'Man! Did you see that?'

'See what?'

'A two-holer.'

'What's a two-holer?'

'An outhouse.'

'You mean an outside toilet?'

'Yeah, man. Usually it's just a one-holer ... y'know, one hole in the seat. And I just saw me a two-holer. Ain't seen one o' those for a while.'

'So what's so special about a two-holer?'

'Yuh get to bring a friend. Yuh can sit side by side while yuh do yer business.'

We get to Birmingham without seeing any two-holers and we collect our passes and make our way backstage. Susie Byrne brings us to where U2's manager, Paul McGuinness, is entertaining guests. Paul makes us very welcome and there is no indication of anything out of the ordinary happening until Paul says, 'You're coming with us tonight, aren't you?'

'Coming where?' I ask.

'Florida.'

'Florida?'

'We're flying to Florida straight after the gig.'

'But I've only the shirt and jeans I'm standing up in,' I splutter.

'They'll do fine.'

Then Susie chips in. 'Paul, the plane is full.'

And this is the bit I really like. Paul says imperiously, 'Bump somebody!'

Suddenly I have a seat, Susie has a problem and Jake has no company for the return journey.

Jake is his usual generous self. 'Go ahead man. It's cool.'

The gig is brilliant. I give Jake a hug and then, as instructed, I take myself backstage as the last number finishes. While the band play a couple of encores, I am ushered into a van and then, as the final chords ring out, the van takes off and we escape the crowds and head for the airport.

I am suitably impressed when we drive out across the tarmac to our aircraft. We board from the rear, walking straight up steps at the back of the plane, with light shining down from inside, just like they did in *Close Encounters of the Third Kind.*

Inside, I am even more impressed. The tail section, on either side, has two red velvet-clad cabanas, which each have two seats facing two more seats. Up ahead of them is a row of regular first-class seats. Then the body opens out into what could well be called a small club. It has a bar about five feet long against one wall. There is a selection of plush, two-seater couches and that's where I find a seat. From where I am sitting I can see forward to the band's quarters, which has a shower and four big individual seats, well spaced out. And up ahead of them, through the open cockpit door, I can see the pilot and co-pilot.

This plane is called the MGM Special. It is a bit like a flying bordello, minus the hookers, and it is used by rock groups and superstars to ferry them around America when they are touring. We sit waiting for take off. The band arrive with a flurry, drenched in sweat. They hurry through to their quarters and the pilot comes on the intercom to instruct us all to take our seats, belt up and remain seated for about ten minutes.

I am not counting, so I don't know for sure, but after what seems like five minutes, everybody stands up and congregates around the bar. Suddenly it's like we are in a nightclub. Bono pours me a glass of champagne and says, 'Champagne for my real friends ... and real pain for my sham friends.' For a split second I wonder if he's paying me a belated compliment for finding him his wedding band – 'a real friend' – and following it with a smack on the wrist for what I said about the band on television – 'a sham friend'.

But one can't be too paranoid with a glass of champagne and good company at 25,000 feet. I have a whale of a time until we are ready to land and then we all resume our seats.

We touch down, taxi to a stop and disembark by the stairs at the rear. Paul says, 'You come with us.' I find myself in a long black limo with Paul and Ellen Darst, the New York-based business woman who takes care of U2's affairs in America. We glide through the dark, out over a long causeway. I can see necklaces of lights on either side, but it is neither the time nor the place to be too nosy, so I keep my beak shut until we pull into the Don Registry Hotel.

In the hotel lobby, I am handed a room key. Because of an hour's time difference between Tennessee and Florida it is now three o'clock in the morning and all is quiet as New Year's Day. I go to my room on the fifth floor, but the notion of going to sleep immediately is impossible. I've just flown with the biggest band in the world, in the swankiest airplane in the world, to a ritzy hotel in Florida. It would be obscene simply to go to bed. I wander back down to the lobby and out to the pool area. There is no sign of the band. A few of the gang from the flight are trying to raise a laugh. One of them walks into the jacuzzi in his suit. It only rates a smile, so after one bottle of beer, I admit defeat and retire.

The hotel literature in my room tells me I am in St Petersburg, Florida. Until that moment, I have never heard of this town. I sleep fitfully and in the morning I approach the reception desk.

'Where am I?'

The receptionist looks at me quizzically. 'You're in St Petersburg.'

'Yes, thank you, I know that. But where is St Petersburg?'

She takes out a map and there is St Petersburg, hanging out on the Gulf of Mexico. All I know of Florida up to now is Miami and Boca Raton on the east coast. To be sure, it is always an adventure to find yourself somewhere new, but I am still in the same shirt and jeans from the night before and it is hot and sticky.

I buy a toothbrush, a razor and a pair of outrageously expensive swimming trunks. I have a swim, put my shirt and jeans back on, thank Paul McGuinness for his hospitality and bid him and U2 adieu.

Now, how the hell do I get back to Nashville from here?

Chapter 2

THE KING AND I

Elvis Presley and I have one thing in common, apart from our good looks. We both had mothers who worshipped us, doted on us and perhaps most critically of all, gave us the kind of encouragement that allowed us to follow our dreams.

Elvis's mother, Gladys, took the death of Elvis's twin, Jesse Garon, at birth as an omen of Elvis's destiny. She was right, and appropriately enough it was when Elvis called in to record two songs for his mother's birthday that the legendary Sam Phillips, owner of Sun Studios in Memphis, first heard him sing.

In 1954, Phillips decided to record Elvis. A desultory, unproductive afternoon recording session was going nowhere until Elvis picked up his guitar and started singing 'That's Alright Mama'. In that moment the world's greatest ever star was born.

Elvis bought his mother a pink Cadillac with his first royalty cheque. All through his career, he would ring his mother at night and talk baby talk down the phone to her. Gladys damaged her liver with her drinking and consequently suffered from chronic hepatitis, which eventually killed her.

Elvis couldn't bear to see his mother ill and when she died, he threw himself on top of her coffin, babbling at her in the strange language that existed only between them.

Like Gladys, my mother spoilt me rotten, often at the expense of my siblings. Of the four girls and two boys in our family, she singled me out above the others for praise and privilege. She was a frustrated writer who wrote stories and plays, but she was forever dragged down by the weight of trying to raise a family of six children on a very small income. When I showed signs of a talent for writing, I think in me she saw a chance to vicariously live out all her dreams.

With her encouragement, at the age of fifteen I took my first faltering steps and wrote an article that was broadcast on Petronella O'Flanagan's afternoon women's programme on RTÉ radio, with myself as the reader. The broadcast went well and I was deliriously happy that I had impressed my mother. At that point, I must have got carried away with myself completely because I then submitted my first article to the Features Editor of a national evening newspaper and he was foolish enough to print it. Frankly, himself and the sub-editor who wrote the headline should both have been taken aside and given a good clip on the ear.

The headline ran: 'I Would Rather Be An Alcoholic Than A Drug Addict.' Let me spare you the drivel and tell you that, mercifully, my fine journalistic mind wasn't called upon again for another couple of years. Then, when I was eighteen and raw out of school, I joined The *Irish Press* Group, as an assistant in the Advertising Features Department.

Advertising features were the bastard child of the news-paper business. When a new pub, shop or hotel opened, the builders and the suppliers would take out ads congratulating the new proprietors. The first stage of my job was to chase the ad reps for the ads. This seemingly innocuous pursuit became the bane of my life. The reps were a bunch of grizzled veterans, who gave me the runaround in no uncertain fashion, to the point that quite often I wound up chasing their ads for them.

I remember once resolving that my third phone call to a dithering prospect named Flood in Donegal would be my final attempt. Surprise, surprise! When he answered, the ditherer had turned into a positive advertiser. I enquired as to what he wanted to say in the ad.

'Okay,' he said. 'Write this down.'

Be it a jig or a reel
A twirl or a twist
A visit to Floods
Cannot be missed.

'That's great,' I enthused. 'So, what size ad would you like?'

'A half inch, single column,' he crowed triumphantly.

That was the smallest ad possible. But the WB Yeats of Donegal sounded so elated with the majesty of his inspired poetry that I let it pass. Who was I to stand in the path of genius?

When I had accomplished the task of assembling the ads, I would then have to chase the man who wrote the article to go with the ads. The writer, J B Meehan, was a retired army man, a stocky, dapper individual who had a penchant for three-piece suits, bow ties, fob watches and suede shoes. He had silver hair and a silver moustache and he oozed refinement through every pore. And even though his job was to write endless amounts of repetitive tosh about flock wallpaper and comfortable banquette seating, he treated his words with the reverence one might afford the Dead Sea Scrolls. For him, writing about the minutiae of lamp fittings and state-of-the-art toilet facilities was nothing less than the committal to print of sacred screeds that, in his mind, would fascinate scholars hundreds of years from now.

I escaped from the newspaper after two years, but just about then there was a tremendous boom in folk music worldwide, and as a devotee of folk music, I became the Folk Correspondent for *Spotlight* magazine, the bible of Irish show business. Now I had a weekly platform from which to air my strident, but fair, opinions. I got so carried away that I even began a Guitar Tutorial, printing the words of popular folk ballads, with diagrams of the guitar chords that went with them.

Alas, hubris was waiting just around the corner. One particular Friday, I gave the layout artist the words and the drawings of the guitar chords. We went to print on Mondays, so I didn't see the finished magazine until Tuesday morning. I opened it at my folk page and when I looked at the diagrams for the guitar chords, I could clearly see that they were not my drawings. Any unfortunate who tried to play these chords would need to be an octopus with elastic fingers. Trembling with rage, I rang the layout man.

'Alan, what the hell happened?'

'Oh, man,' he says, 'I'm really sorry. I lost your diagrams and we were up against our deadline, so I had to remember them as best I could!'

To this day, I feel guilty that I may have been responsible for countless young men and women abandoning their pursuit of a career in music on the basis that the fingering was too difficult. However, I didn't feel bad enough to abandon my column and when I moved to Boston in 1971, I continued to write for *Spotlight* from America. By the time I returned from America in 1975, *Spotlight* was officially gone and in its place was *Starlight*.

I soon found myself with the grandiose title of Associate Editor, which covered a multitude of duties. Firstly, I was a reporter. Secondly, I was a sub-editor. Thirdly, I was a layout man. And fourthly, I was a staff writer, along with one other. He would write the 'Letters To The Editor' one week, and I would respond. The following week we would swap roles. If only the editor had known.

Starlight was operating on a shoestring and in those pre-Internet days when research was an arduous task, it required great ingenuity to fill its pages. That was when I first started feeling close to Elvis. I would buy magazines like *Modern Screens Gems* and *Hollywood News* and from them I would cull a couple of interviews with Elvis. I would begin by cutting out all the quotes and spreading them out on the floor. Then I would reassemble them and in the process concoct a wide-ranging interview with The King, with all the authority of a man who had just stepped off a plane from Memphis. And Elvis always mentioned his mother.

Had I been able to see into the future, I would have seen that this gathering up of Elvis trivia was to be invaluable to me. And many people believed that I *could* see into the future, after all, wasn't I a dab hand at the horoscopes in *Starlight?*

Initially, I set about fulfilling my obligation as a weekly clairvoyant with great diligence, by actually writing generalised and bogus prognostications for each star sign. But as well as fooling the public, I was only fooling myself and even though I enjoyed promising great things to those in my own star sign, Aries, the task quickly palled. It was much easier to buy a girl's comic called *Jackie* and copy their horoscopes. All I had to do was change the typefaces to suit our printers. And here was the pay-off: each week subsequently I just moved the star signs around. I gave Pisces to Virgo, Aries to Saggitarius, Capricorn to Gemini. Nobody ever complained.

Just because they didn't complain about the horoscopes, it didn't mean there weren't other complaints. As our circulation shrank, so too did our number of contributors. We had an advice column called 'Dear Mary' and when the writer quit, the bookkeeper took over. She was a good bookkeeper but her flair for writing was in numbers only. The writing of the agony column fell to my fellow staff writer, a worldly-wise young man, with liberal leanings and a breezy attitude to sex.

A young man wrote to Mary and the gist of his letter was this:

'Dear Mary,
I masturbate a lot. Recently I have noticed angry red
weals on my penis. Could this be a venereal disease?
Anxious, Kilkenny.'

Mary replied:

'Dear Anxious,
Stop worrying. You cannot get a venereal disease from
masturbating. These angry red weals are nothing more
than friction burns.'

The phones exploded. Rabid parish priests and incandescent, angry mothers of seven wanted to know what kind of advice we were dispensing to the youth of the nation? It didn't matter that our man was on the money with his diagnosis. He was relieved of his duties as Agony Aunt, forthwith.

My favourite interviewee, Elvis, died on 16 August 1977. I was profoundly sad that the life of such a beautiful and talented singer had become warped in the cocoon of unreality that his manager had spun for him. Even worse, in that bubble he was surrounded by loyal but unsophisticated henchmen who knew nothing other than watching over Elvis, pandering to his every whim and in some cases feeding off the sexual crumbs that fell from Elvis's table.

A couple of days after his death, I was reading about Elvis and thinking back over all the stories I had written about him, when the phone rang. It was Ireland's premier theatre impresario of the time, Noel Pearson, who was planning to stage a musical about Elvis, called *The King*. Would I be interested in writing the script? And could he have it tomorrow? I looked out my front door and, noticing the absence of a queue of people waiting to give me work, I agreed to do it on the spot.

The creative juices in me started pumping immediately. Not alone did I know all kinds of trivial details about Elvis Aaron Presley, I also knew all about his dead twin, Jesse Garon, about his child-bride Priscilla, about his affair with Juliet Prowse, about his last girlfriend, Ginger, about his Dad, Vernon, about his clingy mother, Gladys, about the pink Cadillac, about the strange baby talk. And to gild the lily, I had lived in Tennessee for two years and I was familiar with that Southern trailer-trash milieu that was his background.

Furthermore, I understood the artistic side of his life. I had been a performer myself – a singer who, one night in Nashville in 1975, had even been backed on stage by one of Elvis's bass players, Norbert Putnam. On the face of it, I was an inspired choice.

I pulled on my jacket and set off walking. I walked up hill and down dale, hearing Elvis talking inside my head, first as a young man and then as the bloated parody of his once beautiful self. I was oblivious to people and to traffic, running speeches in my head, imagining the voice of his mother Gladys echoing in his head in his sad, final moments. For four hours I traversed the streets and avenues of Blackrock and Mount Merrion and then I went home and wrote it all down.

The King opened in the Olympia Theatre in Dublin on 21 November 1977, just three months after Elvis died, creating its own bit of history as the first posthumous stage musical in the world about Elvis. My mother would have been proud. A showband singer named Cahir O'Doherty captured all the energy of the young Elvis, and one of Ireland's greatest actors ever, Donal McCann, played the mumbling, overweight shambles who died ignobly at just forty-two, sitting on the toilet.

The only blot on my proud landscape was caused by finding out by accident that a Belfast journalist named Donal Corvin who had written alongside me for *Spotlight* all those years ago, had originally been asked to write the script, but had fallen off the radar into a bottle and gone missing. Which is where I came in, thinking I was an inspired choice.

Inspired choice, my ass.

Wherever you are Elvis, I bet you're smiling.

Chapter 3

THE PECKER

The first time I laid eyes on The Pecker Dunne, I was absolutely mesmerised. He had a big head and a face that looked like it was chiselled from granite. He was a cross between Zorba The Greek and Geronimo, the legendary Red Indian chief. His magnificent head of hair – a vast tangle of black, oily ringlets and curls – cascaded down to his shoulders and in the dim light of the Jug of Punch pub in Kilkenny, plucking his banjo and singing his anthem 'Sullivan's John', he looked fierce and forbidding.

The Jug of Punch was owned at the time by Liam Clancy, one of the famous singing Clancy Brothers from Carrick-on-Suir. As the evening wore on, Liam introduced me to The Pecker, who was, Liam explained, a famous busker. To my great surprise I found a mannerly, soft-spoken man, diffident and amusing. I listened to him, fascinated, as he told me stories of growing up in Wexford and of his life as a traveller on the road in a horse-drawn caravan.

When I knew him better, I ventured one day to ask about a circular indentation, the size of an old penny and about an eighth of an inch deep, on his large forehead. I don't know to this day if he was putting me on or not, but he solemnly answered, 'Me father hit me with a hammer because I wouldn't practise the fiddle.'

The Pecker became a good friend and I grew used to seeing him suddenly materialise in the most unlikely places. I'd be doing a gig in Ballybunion and he would be there. Then I'd find myself in Clonmel and who would be there again, larger than life, but The Pecker. The folk boom of the Sixties was in full blossom and almost inevitably, The Pecker came under the scrutiny of Tribune Records, which was owned by Noel Pearson, Mick Quinn and Robert McGrattan. Tribune had a hot stable of folk acts and everybody said that, with a bit of guidance, The Pecker could be huge.

The Pecker was deemed a star-in-waiting and the showcase for his unique talent was to be a show called The Gatecrashers, produced by Noel Pearson at the Gate theatre. It was no more than a glorified folk concert but, I think because my father was an actor, I was listed as being the nominal director.

There wasn't much direction involved. I was the host of the show, introducing folk stalwart Al O'Donnell, and Danny Doyle, who was a big star on the back of two hit singles, 'Step It Out Mary' and 'Whiskey On A Sunday'. The Pecker was top of the bill. Photographer Tom Collins, who now works as a stills photographer on major movies, brought The Pecker, Danny and myself to the back garden of a house in Rathmines Road in Dublin and Tom took photos of the three of us peering out through a tangle of waist-high weeds. The Gatecrashers album sleeve is a work of art, a work apart.

The opening night in the Gate was a lively affair. The folkerrati were to the forefront in their tweeds and sandals, mingling comfortably with legitimate theatregoers and curious onlookers. The night went smoothly and, with his head held high and his shoulders thrown back, The Pecker effortlessly stole the show. After many curtain calls, I took off my make-up, hung my new Bri-nylon shirt on a hook on the wall of my dressing room and retired with the cast and crew to Groome's Hotel, just across from the theatre. Groome's was a den of artistic iniquity, where actors, artists, writers, journalists, chancers and fantasists of the day lied and boasted to each other with gay and straight abandon.

Good reviews next day put a lively spring in our step, but suddenly the day was gone and at fifteen minutes to curtain there was no sign of The Pecker. An air of panic began to permeate the theatre as the hunt went on for the missing star. Meanwhile, backstage, I was having a smaller personal crisis. The brand new Bri-nylon shirt I had bought specially for the show was missing from its hook. I scoured the theatre up and down, checking every dressing-room, toilet and cubby hole, but no trace of my precious shirt could I find. The crisis with The Pecker eventually superseded the worry of my missing shirt and I joined an anxious producer in speculating on where he might be.

With the clock now at five to eight, it looked ominous. There could be no show without The Pecker. I decided to have one last look up the street and as I stepped out onto the pavement and looked left up the hill, around the top of Parnell Square came a horse and cart, travelling at a good lick, a young traveller at the reins and The Pecker sitting up beside him like King George III on his royal visit to Dublin. He had a broad grin across his big, wide face and – wait for it – my lovely Bri-nylon shirt tied in a knot across his expansive belly!

The Pecker could do no wrong. He became really hip, appearing in New York to adoring crowds, hob-nobbing with The Dubliners and being invited as the star guest to every fleadh and session in Ireland. Surely he would soon be a superstar?

But it never happened. The gigs came rolling in and for a while The Pecker enjoyed the taste of celebrity, but my own theory is that inevitably the glamour began to pall and the idea of being tied to a diary and having to show up in definite places at definite times became too much for our knight-of-the-road. Pecker went back to the thing he knew best, busking.

On a dull, grey morning in September 1967, when myself and Dymphna Errity stepped out of Ballyfermot church as the new Mr and Mrs Shay Healy, The Pecker was waiting for us, dressed in a green anorak and a white shirt, his banjo around his neck, serenading us with a tune as we took our first faltering steps as a married couple. It was a generous and much appreciated gesture.

We finally left the church grounds and drove out to the wedding breakfast. A couple of hundred yards from Mick McCarthy's famous pub, The Embankment, we stopped and took a right turn up a back road and transferred to a donkey and cart, on which we then rode majestically into the car park of The Embankment, into a waiting flurry of photographers.

Dymphna's outfit was stunning, She looked as if she had been spun from pure gossamer, and she was bathed in a creamy glow that was light and delicate. She had just alighted from the donkey and cart, when suddenly, from behind a row of parked cars, The Pecker emerged, roaring like a bull, his aim to snatch up the confection that was Dymphna and carry her off. She ran as fast as she could, with The Pecker in hot pursuit and me trying to get between The Pecker and my bride.

The chase seemed to go on forever. My heart was pounding. I was getting tired. The Pecker was inches from my bride when I heard the cry, 'Cut'. My friend Paddy Lockhart turned off his cine camera and gave us the thumbs-up. 'Worked a treat,' he said. I still have our movie. Much later, Pecker appeared in a film called *Trojan Eddie* with Richard Harris, but when we haul out our wedding movie for the craic, we still believe it is without doubt The Pecker's finest thespian moment.

The Pecker stayed with us all day. Mick McCarthy gave us a deal on a 'glass of sherry and chicken in the basket' for the guests, and his favourable rate allowed us to invite loads of friends as well as family. The roguish Mick also laid on the donkey and cart. It was the generous gesture of a friend, but I could also be sure that Mick knew the value of a photograph of the Embankment on the front page of the *Evening Press*.

The sherry worked. We had a mighty session, with The Pecker in the thick of it, and I had such a good time that my last memory of the wedding breakfast was of myself standing on a table, still singing at 11.25pm on my wedding night!

One day, years later, I got a call from Mervyn Solomons, head of Emerald Records in Belfast. Mervyn's syrupy voice, which had only a tiny hint of Belfast, came oozing down the phone. 'I'd like you to produce an album with Pecker Dunne.' I instantly agreed and in jig time I was in Belfast recording with The Pecker. Remarkably, it was his first album, but with no pre-production or rehearsal, it was going to be a bit rough. Pecker's banjo style belongs with a busker and not in a studio.

To add to my woes, I had three other musicians – two Catholics who were not great and a Protestant who was a wizard. We had to smuggle the Protestant in and out of Homestead Studios in the boot of a car because the politics of the time in Northern Ireland were such that this combination of Teagues and Prods would not be looked upon too favourably by either side.

We recorded and mixed the album in three days. The Pecker delivered his own impeccable style with gusto, and the album, 'Introducing The Pecker Dunne', was duly mixed and made ready to launch the recording career of one of Ireland's great characters. We sat in Mervyn

Solomons's office. 'Now, Pecker,' he said. 'I can give you a recording royalty of fifteen percent, which you will get in six months to a year's time, or I can give you six hundred pounds cash, now.'

'I'll take the money, sir,' sez The Pecker.

The mid-Nineties was the last time I met The Pecker in the flesh. I had him as a guest on a nostalgia television show I was doing at the time. The Pecker was by now sporting a grey beard and the fabulous, black, oily mane of his youth had turned almost white. But to look at him, he was still a one-off in every way, proud to tell me that the music in his family goes back two hundred years. He now had a marionette of himself, replete with banjo, which he bounced up and down on a stick as he entertained the crowd on their way to the Munster Hurling Final in Thurles, or to see Kerry play Dublin in Killarney.

Pecker told me that after a long time on the road, in everything from horse-drawn caravans to an endless series of vans, he had eventually settled in a house in Killimer, in the rolling West Clare countryside.

'Pecker,' I asked him, 'How do you feel about being settled?'

'Well, d'ye know what it is,' sez Pecker, 'I don't know how a man can look out the window and see the *one* tree every day of his life!'

Chapter 4

JUSTIN TIME

When you are gigging as a solo act, there is more required of you than a talent for singing and telling jokes. You have to be able to get paid, to get the money without having to wait for two hours while the pub or club owner farts around looking busy, deliberately avoiding eye contact.

The greatest story of collecting the gig money belongs with Ben Dolan, bandleader of Joe Dolan and The Drifters, one of Ireland's superstar bands of the golden era of Irish showbands in the 1960s. Joe and The Drifters were playing at a ballroom in the West of Ireland. The promoter of the dance was a priest, which was not at all unusual back in those days. All over Ireland there were entrepreneurial clerics, men in black, with an eye on the half-chance, not afraid to use their power and position in society to dabble in the arena of showbiz.

Ben's band was, according to the story, on a guaranteed fee of one thousand pounds for the night. The crowd was smaller than anticipated and at the end of the night the priest came to Ben, a bundle of notes rolled up in his hand.

'There's eight hundred pounds there, Ben. We had a bad night.'

Ben looked him levelly in the eye. 'Put another two hundred pounds to that, Father. There's no point in us all having a bad night!'

Just recounting that story still gives me a bit of a thrill, a satisfaction that for once, one of our guys got the upper hand. On behalf of us all, Ben has become a totem and whenever we gather to retell our favourite stories, Ben's great moment always gets an airing.

There were many nights when I had to hang around after a gig, sometimes for as much as an hour. It seemed as though the proprietors of these pubs and cabaret lounges took a perverse delight in leaving you squirming, almost begging for the money you had honestly earned. And when you did get the money, they tried to make you feel like you were taking the crust out of their children's mouths. They would invariably trot out a wearyingly familiar list of moans: 'There wasn't much of a crowd in tonight,' 'Yer posters never arrived in time,' followed by, 'Will ya be givin' me back a luck penny?'

The trickiest collection of the money that ever happened me took place in a big pub in the south of Ireland. I'm not being coy, but there's no point in trashing the guy's name at this far remove, so I will call him Justin and not tell you the name of the pub.

When I arrive and see the size of the room I will be singing in, my heart sinks. All I have with me is a 100-watt sound rig, not nearly enough for a place this size. It is going to be a struggle, with just me and a guitar against the world. I fortify myself with a vodka and then I launch myself into this Coliseum full of culchies – a Christian with only a guitar for a weapon, while the lions of doubt snap at my heels.

It's a tough one. I'm thirty minutes in and just about holding my own. It will be a miracle if I can stretch this to the hour they are expecting. But sometimes the gods give you deliverance unexpectedly and my salvation comes in the shape of a shout from the back of the room.

'Get Justin up to sing.'

The single voice is quickly joined by a chorus, which grows rapidly to a small chant: 'We want Justin. We want Justin.'

Justin, the proprietor, is moving amongst the tables, picking up empty glasses and affecting a damn fine display of modesty.

'Ah no, I won't,' he says diffidently.

The pantomime actor in me takes over.

'Oh yes, you will,' I hector good-humouredly. 'C'mon Justin. They want you.'

Justin is wavering. A few more exhortations over the mike and suddenly Justin is mine, standing beside me at the mike. Justin is about five feet nine inches, the beginnings of a belly in evidence under the waistcoat and trousers of his brown tweed suit. His hair is thinning into a potential comb-over special of the future, but he has a kindly face and a ready smile and I have a feeling that underneath the reluctance he probably is genuinely a bit shy and not really vain.

I'm wrong, of course. Mr Modest has absconded. Justin is a monster and promptly tells me that he'll sing 'just a couple'. With great relief I find out that his repertoire stretches to well-known Irish parlour songs, most of which I can cover with my barely adequate guitar playing. I give him a huge build-up, candyfloss spun from meaningless, sugary clichés and then he launches off into Thomas Moore's 'Love Thee Dearest'. And, surprise, surprise, Justin sings in a very commendable, light tenor voice.

The crowd loves it. I love it. Another five minutes have been lopped off the hour.

'Another song from Justin,' I shout.

'More, more,' the punters chorus.

Justin sings a second song. The end of my torment is another four minutes closer. But now Justin is intent on finishing. It is time for a bit of obsequiousness.

'Ladies and gentlemen,' I say, ' I have performed all over Ireland, but I have never experienced anything like the pleasure of working for a man with such a fine voice.'

My calculated gamble pays off. Hubris keeps Justin at the microphone and he finishes off with a humourous Percy French song, 'McBreen's Heifer'. Tumultuous applause. Much bowing.

Justin is a hero for singing. And I am a hero for being so generous as to allow him be part of my act. Only fifteen minutes to go now. I hit them with my killer material and whilst I wouldn't describe it as a resounding victory, I earn a very respectable draw.

Relieved and happy, I retire to the front room-cum-office, where a plate of cold ham and tomatoes awaits me. By osmosis, all over Ireland, cold ham and tomatoes had become the culinary reward for artistes and musicians, whatever the weather, winter and summer. We never found the godhead responsible for determining what post-gig food should be, but I would not be surprised to find that ham and tomatoes is still number one on the list today.

Anyway, having finished my cold ham and tomatoes, I go back into the lounge and break down my speakers and my amp. All the while I am clocking Justin as he moves amongst the tables, collecting glasses, ducking behind the bar, shaking hands with punters. Soon it will be time to engage in the grisly *pas-de-deux* of getting paid.

The gear is safely packed in the car, so I wander in to the fringe of the room. Justin is busy doing everything conceivable except looking in my direction. He passes at a distance of a couple of tables.

'Justin,' I call out.

'I'll be witcha in a minit,' he shouts back.

Now the duel is really on. Several more times he passes, sometimes close, sometimes far away, but never again does he give me a chance to engage him eye-to-eye. It's now past midnight, the gear is stowed in the car and a one-hundred-and-forty-mile drive through soft drizzle awaits me outside. Desperate measures are called for. He is only two tables away.

'Justin ... your VOICE!'

Justin stops. He is snagged when he hears the word 'voice'. He comes towards me.

'What are ye sayin' to me?'

'Your voice,' I say earnestly. 'I am amazed to hear such a good singer who isn't doing it for a living.'

He is up like a salmon, gobbling my compliments as he

comes to my side. The hook is in.

'Thank you very much. I did think about it once. Y'know I won a big competition in Cork about ten years ago and I could have gone on because the prize was a kind of scholarship.'

'I'm not surprised to hear you won something,' I gush.

And then a kind of wistful smile begins to play on Justin's lips. His soft face takes on the rueful sadness of a martyr.

'But it was no good. It was never going to work out.'

It was never going to work out? What was never going to work out? What was the mystery that had come between Justin and his destiny as a tenor?

'Justin, why was it never going to work out?'

'I'll tell you the truth,' he whispers without a trace of irony. 'I ruined my voice in the pub here, shouting, "TIME GENTLEMEN PLEASE".'

There is no answer to that. But small things like that have never stopped me before.

'Well, the world has been cheated out of a great singer,' I say, as Justin hands me my fee, a bundle of notes rolled up with an elastic band. Job done. Money safe in pocket.

Relieved and proud of my collecting strategy, I extricate myself from Justin's company with one last compliment and a firm handshake. And then I am off on my long, lonely journey into the wet, black night.

Roll on the lights of Dublin City.

Chapter 5

CHUCK IS IN LOVE

In 1971, I moved to a small town called Norwood in Massachussets, about fourteen miles out from Boston on Route I. You could have knocked me down with a feather when, one day, I spotted a small ad in the local paper saying that Chuck Berry would be appearing in the gym at Dedham High School the following Monday. Dedham was the next town up the line. This would be an unmissable rock 'n' roll gig.

John Lennon said, 'If you tried to give rock 'n' roll another name, you might call it Chuck Berry.' How right he was. Chuck Berry is a fascinating character. Born on the right side of the tracks in St Louis, Missouri, he and his family lived in The Ville, just north of downtown, the first prosperous black community in the city. His mother was a teacher and his father was an Archdeacon in Antioch Baptist Church.

In 1944, when he was just eighteen, Chuck and two companions were arrested on a joyride to Kansas City. They were convicted of armed robbery. As a result of this brush with the law, he spent eight years in the clink. In 1952 he started played music and he got his first big break in 1955 when his song 'Maybellene' sold over one million copies.

But success was tempered with anger and disappointment when he found out that, whether he liked it or not, he was sharing the writing credits with Russ Fratto and Alan Freed, the legendary DJ who had made 'Maybellene' a hit. At the same time, Chuck discovered that his agent was pocketing some of his fees. From that moment on, Chuck resolved that self-sufficiency would be the key to his survival.

A string of hits over the next few years stamped Chuck as one of the great rock 'n' roll writers of all time: 'Too Much Monkey Business', 'Rock 'n' Roll Music', 'Sweet Little Sixteen', 'Johnny B. Goode', 'Roll Over Beethoven'. But by 1962, he was back in jail for three years, convicted this time of 'transporting a woman across State lines for immoral purposes'.

They could lock up Chuck, but they couldn't lock up his music. With The Beatles covering 'Roll Over Beethoven' and 'Rock 'n' Roll Music', Chuck's legendary status was now established in Europe as well as America. While in jail he wrote 'No Particular Place To Go' and a string of other hits, but when he left the family-owned Chess Records in 1966 and signed to Mercury, his recording career went into decline. In 1972, he had one last spectacular comeback with the bawdy 'My Ding-A-Ling', a rude, jokey song, which was less than vintage Chuck. His career as a top recording artist was pretty much over, but as a performer, there was a lot more left in the bag.

Chuck, Elvis, Bill Haley and their ilk were my heroes growing up in Dublin the 1950s, and although I later became a bit of a folkie, I survived the Swinging Sixties by keeping one ear permanently cocked for American music. When he came 'riding along' in his automobile, I had no control over my atavistic compulsion to dance. Myself and my sister Emer even won the jiving competition in Railway Union Tennis Club. I was hot stuff.

I never fell out of love with Chuck Berry. If he was good enough for The Beatles, he was good enough for me, and over the passing years, I kept abreast of him in a generalised way, reading snippets about him in music magazines and hearing his evergreen songs constantly on the radio.

I had read that Chuck had worked out a breathtakingly audacious *modus operandum* that was arrogant, but obvious. He would turn up for a gig and use local musicians as his band. Chuck's repertoire of hits was so great and so all-pervasive that any rock 'n' roll musician worth his salt would be able to play 'Johnny B. Goode', 'Roll Over Beethoven' and all of Chuck's other hits without the tedium of having to rehearse. It was Chuck's philosophy of self-sufficiency at its ultimate best. No manager. No agent. Turn up. Do the gig. Get the money. And scram.

The gig in Dedham High School is brilliant. I feel like I am an extra on the set of *Grease*. The girls have ponytails. The boys have their High School baseball jackets and blue jeans. The iconography of teenage America is all around me in a plain old gymnasium. There is no fancy lighting and the amplification is minimal. I am totally seduced by the whole picture. It smells of primal rock 'n' roll and Chuck's logic in using local musicians is inspired. The band can hardly believe they are playing with a legend, and consequently everybody plays out of their skins.

After the gig I wander round backstage, totally elated. I am still writing an occasional interview for *Spotlight* magazine back in Ireland. Getting an interview with Chuck would be a fair old scoop. I approach the great man's door and knock. Chuck opens the door and behind him in his dressing room, I can see a vampy-looking, blonde, white woman. I introduce myself and request an interview.

'Gimme a couple of minits,' says the great man.

Also waiting outside Chuck's dressing room is a fifteen-year-old kid. As the minutes drag by without any sign of Chuck reappearing, I begin conversing with him. He tells me his story.

'I was hitching a ride on Route 128 to come and see this gig, man, when a big car pulled in with a man and a woman in it. The man asked me where I was going and I told him I was going to see Chuck Berry at Dedham High. He didn't say anything else and the next thing I know we're pulling into the parking lot here. We get out of the car and then, man, I can't believe it … it's Chuck Berry. Man, the dude who's drivin' the car is Chuck Berry!'

My new young pal is hoping to get a ride back into Boston with his hero. We talk about how great the gig was; and time is now dragging on … and on. I wait for about another twenty minutes before I decide to knock on the door and get an update. I rap gently on the door and to my horror, the door swings open to reveal my hero Chuck, sitting on a chair, his vampy blonde sitting on his knee.

Chuck whirls around angrily. 'What you doin'?'

'I'm really sorry,' I apologise. 'I didn't expect the door to open.'

'What you want?'

'D'you remember? I'm the guy from Ireland who wanted to do an interview with you.'

'Yeah, yeah! I'll be out in a minit.'

Mortified, I return to my seat. Five more minutes pass and then Chuck opens the door and comes out.

'Okay,' Chuck says. 'Ya have three questions.'

'Are you serious?'

Chuck looks at me, cold and unsmiling.

'That's one!'

Chapter 6

DON'T MESS WITH THE MOB

On my very first night in New York, I appeared in Carnegie Hall. Impressive or what!

The reality is that it isn't that impressive. I am to be master of ceremonies at a concert starring the Irish rebel ballad group, the Wolfe Tones, and ex-Dublin firefighter Jesse Owens and his performing partner, box player James Keane. Topping the bill is the recently-split-from-the-Clancy-Brothers Tommy Makem. I am hooked into the promoters, so I get the gig via my connections, rather than on any special merit.

I have flown in on the shuttle from Boston to La Guardia airport early in the morning. I am agog with excitement. My first view of the New York skyline is close to orgasmic – a familiar sight, courtesy of a million movies. The cacophony of car horns, the sound of the subway rumbling below, the steam rising from the vents in the street, the smell of fresh bread, satisfies all my senses and surpasses all my expectations. It feels like I am in someone else's video. I shamelessly crane my neck with all the gaucheness of a country hick, but it isn't until we are installed in a twelfth-floor office on Madison Avenue, that I realise that it is the girth and not the height of the buildings that is so impressive. Big fat buildings, big fat skyscrapers.

Outside Carnegie Hall there is a poster for the gig. As a late addition, my name isn't on the poster, but I hide my disappointment. After all, I am here in Carnegie Hall, the Everest of performance halls, the apex, the apogee, the zenith, the venue that requires such a difficult climb if one is to reach its hallowed stage. And here I am, without the aid of Sherpas or oxygen.

There are no curtains in Carnegie Hall. My first entrance calls for a cold and lonely walk from the wings out to the microphone centre-stage. I can hear the echo of my footsteps on the wooden floor and a clammy hand has my guts in a fine twist as I pray I won't trip and fall. In my hand I have a lyric sheet belonging to the Wolfe Tones, which I am to put on a music stand in front of the mike. I get as far as the mike and as I put the sheet of paper on the music stand, it slips from my fingers and begins falling towards the floor. Everything goes into slow motion. The sheet of paper falls like a leaf in autumn, languidly scything from side to side. I watch in horror and make a grab for it and miss. When it finally settles on the floor, I pick it up between a trembling forefinger and thumb and glance up at the audience. Every eye is on me.

'That's a great start to my first appearance in Carnegie Hall,' I quip.

They laugh. That's all I need to hear. I am off and running.

Next day I am high as a kite on my previous night's success. I can hardly wait to get at another audience, so when I am introduced to Tom Murray, who has booked me to sing in New Jersey on this the eve of St Patrick's Day, I am full of chat and banter as we leave New York behind and head for his home in West Orange.

Tom is one of those big, loud, roundy Irish-Americans – six-foot-three, no neck, all shoulders, belly and bum. His broad face is starting to melt slowly into his body. Naturally, it transpires that he has played football at school. Tom owns an Irish pub and he talks it up a storm on the way to his handsome house in a very salubrious neighbourhood. His has fine big home, with well-proportioned rooms, including a panelled library and a grand staircase. Tom is obviously not without a few dollars. I immediately assume that if his house is this nice, the pub will, in all probability, be as nice, if not nicer.

A couple of hours later, when we are driving to the pub, Tom begins to tell me, in a long, slow whine, that the pub is struggling a bit. And then, in an incredibly matter-of-fact way, he blithely informs me that the Mafia is trying to take it over. And as if that isn't enough, he further informs me that the FBI has fitted him with a 'wire' so that they can listen in to his conversations with the Mob.

'Will *they* be here tonight?' My query emerges as a frightened squeak.

'I don't know,' comes the gruff reply.

Great. Just great. My first night in New York is a Carnegie Hall triumph and a day later I get killed by the Mob. Probably in the middle of 'Danny Boy'.

The rest of the drive is conducted in silence. When we reach the pub, there are very few customers. It is very definitely a neighbourhood place. The oval-shaped bar is just inside the door. The performance area is up a couple of steps. It is wide enough and long enough to hold about 120 people. The stage is up another level again.

I follow Tom up the steps, across the stage and into an office behind. When we get inside, Tom takes off his gabardine trench coat, pulls out a gun and something that looks like a walkie-talkie from the inside pocket and reaches up and deposits them on top of a metal locker. I am wide-eyed and speechless.

'Now,' he advises me, deadpan, 'If I come up to you and say we're getting out of here, even if you're in the middle of a song, you're to come with me.'

'What do you mean?'

'Just do what I tell ya.'

My instinct is to tell him I am leaving, *now*, but his look tells me that argument is futile. Besides, I haven't a clue where I am, apart from knowing that I am somewhere in New Jersey.

'Don't forget what I told ya about leaving.'

I nod dumbly in agreement. Tom exits, leaving me alone in the office to do some solitary quaking. What have I done to myself? How come my big promoter pal in New York hadn't filled me in on Tom's situation? Did he know? Questions, questions, questions.

At 8.30pm I strap on my guitar, step from the office onto the stage and begin singing. There are a couple of guys drinking at the bar who look innocuous enough. I scan every new punter that comes in. Do they have suits with big shoulders? Do they look dark and swarthy? The small smattering of punters in the performance area appears not to give a hoot about me for the half-hour I stay on stage. I finish singing and retreat into the office, my heart in my boots. I sit and sit, not knowing what to do, until I reckon it is time to go on again for my second set. Once more I make the lonely walk to the mike at centre-stage, wistfully remembering the splendour of Carnegie Hall and an audience that cared.

Just as I begin singing, two softball teams make a postgame, noisy entrance, some of them still in their baseball gear. That puts paid to any prospects of witty patter, so I concentrate on singing up-tempo songs, ever watchful for the arrival of possible gangsters. And then I suddenly become conscious of Tom at the bar, engaged in animated conversation with two guys. In the gloom of the bar their features are hidden from me, but from the vigour of the nodding and shaking of heads, it appears to be a spirited exchange of views.

Then Tom detaches himself from the conversation and comes walking towards the stage. As he passes me on his way into the office, he says, 'Let's go,' from the corner of his mouth.

I stop in mid-song and, surprise, surprise, nobody seems to notice. However, this is no time to become affronted by punter indifference. This might be a matter of life and death.

In the office Tom is reaching on top of the locker for the gun and a device that looks like a flat microphone. He throws the device to me.

'Put that in your guitar case.'

'What is it?' Another squeaky question escapes my lips.

'It's a listening device. It belongs to the FBI.'

Then he takes his coat and, holding the gun in a firing position in his right hand, he drapes the coat over his arm so that the gun isn't visible. As I follow him out the door, my brain is stuck in a no-man's land between horrified and terrified. We climb down off the stage, walk through the bar and out into the parking lot. I prudently avoid looking left or right. We climb into his car and he screeches out of the car park and takes off at speed. My heart is going at a rate of knots.

But the rapid heartbeat is nothing compared to the quickening that follows Tom's sudden utterance.

'Uh-oh!'

'Don't tell me "uh-oh" means we're being followed?' I implore.

'I think so.'

We skitter around corners for the next fifteen minutes. Headlights loom menacingly in the wing mirror and then, just as I anticipate that they are going to draw abreast of us and force us off the road, they peel away. I have no idea whether there really is somebody following us or not and I feel no sense of relief as we pull into Tom's driveway. They could bump us off here just as easily as outside the pub.

'What do we do?' I squeak for the third time.

'You'd better go to bed.'

I climb the stairs to the room I am sleeping in. It is approximately 9.50pm I haven't been in bed this early since I was about six years old. Through some miracle, there is a copy of *Time* magazine in my room. I devour it, but every small creak in the house gives me a start.

I fall into an uneasy asleep, only to be startled awake by a loud knocking on the front door. I glance at my watch. It is almost midnight. I jump from my bed, tiptoe over to the door and pull it open just a crack. Tom is walking down the stairs, his gun stuck out in front of him in his right hand.

We'll all be shot in our beds, I think to myself.

Tom reaches the front door. 'Who is it?' he shouts.

And then from outside the door come the sweetest three words I have ever heard.

'It's the FBI.'

Tom opens the door and two men in suits step into the hall. He leads them into the library and closes the door, so that I am unable to hear any more. I try staying awake, but the nervous exhaustion gets the better of me and I nod off.

When I wake next morning to find myself still alive, I am mighty relieved. I shun the notion of breakfast and don't hesitate for a second when Tom suggests we head back into New York. In fairness to him, despite my truncated appearance the night before, he pays me my agreed fee without demur. There is little chat on the journey. The ebullient Tom of the outward journey has given way to a sullen, brooding presence, and, operating on the basis of the old adage that discretion is the better part of valour, I never bring up the goings-on of the night before. When at last we emerge from the Lincoln tunnel into Manhattan I feel the tension finally ooze out of my body. Manhattan will never look as good again.

At the corner of 52nd Street and Madison Avenue, Tom pulls over to the kerb. I drag my guitar from the back seat, shake his hand and bid him farewell. And as his car gets swallowed up in a sea of yellow cabs, I heave a huge sigh of relief and surrender myself to the warm glow of the New York bustle.

Chapter 7

TARA-RA-BOOM-DI-AY

Tara Restaurant and Bar at the junction of 21st Avenue and Broadway in Nashville, Tennessee, opens without fanfare on 6 June 1973. We are expecting the name to work on two levels. For those who are just plain old Southerners, Tara is the name of the estate in the movie *Gone With The Wind*. And for those who know their Irish history, Tara was the ancient seat of the High Kings of Ireland.

Across the street is Ireland's Restaurant, a place whose Irishness ends with the shamrock on their logo. But Tara is the Real McCoy, Music City's first genuine Irish bar. And I am the Head Leprechaun and sole entertainer.

It's a long wait for our first customer and then, at eight o'clock, a guy called Ralph finally stumbles in and earns that distinction. We smother him with gratitude and free drink. At 8.30pm I climb on to the stage, plug in my guitar and give my audience of one a half-hour of Irish ballads and jokes. He likes it.

Presently a young couple arrives. They are bubbling over with good humour and a bit of quizzing reveals that they have tied the knot just hours before. We break open a bottle of champagne and toast the happy couple in style, along the way sucking our first customer Ralph into the company.

At 9.15 I get back up on stage and sing for another half-hour, interspersing the songs with gags and banter between me and the newly-weds. We are all having a good time and Ralph orders a cocktail called a Side Car. It is our first sale.

By ten o'clock Ralph is ready to jack it in, so we shower him with benedictions and send him off into the night. But the newly-weds are going nowhere. Once again I plug in and this time I am singing to an audience of two, who are showing no signs of quitting. As I start into my final number of the set, I say to them over the mike, 'Isn't there something better you could be doing rather than sitting here listening to some Irish wacko telling jokes?' They laugh like a drain. As opening nights go, what it lacks in fireworks, it makes up for in enthusiasm.

My arrival in Nashville had been as spontaneous as almost everything else I had done before or since. I had been back living in Dublin after singing for a year in Boston, when Mike Brodbine, one of the Bostonians I had worked for, arrived in Dublin and posed the question, 'Do you want to go to Nashville and be my partner?' Exercising my incisive propensity for longterm planning, I answered, 'When?'

Two months later I am flying into Nashville, not knowing what to expect. I am remarkably naive, expecting to find that Nashville is a hick town, with wooden storefronts and wooden boardwalks, and rails where a man might tether his horse. It is a bit of a surprise to find that Nashville is a modern city, still mercifully free of high-rise buildings, but firmly in the twentieth century.

Back in Dublin I had carved out a reputation as a writer of folk songs, so the prospect of being in Nashville, with so many songwriters, is tremendously exciting. But, if anything, I am even more naive when I expect the fabled Music Row of Nashville to be a down-homey cabbage patch full of guys with guitars and banjos sitting around writing songs. Music Row encompasses all the streets and avenues from 12th Avenue to 20th Avenue and each one of these avenues has music studios cheek-by-jowl with record companies, music publishers, restaurants and bars.

Thankfully, I am quick to assimilate. I am much taken by the courtesy and polite charm that are in abundance and once I get used to the Southern twang, I settle quickly. The heat is murderously humid, but we flog the builders and Tara gradually takes shape. The mostly wooden building was once a fraternity house attached to Vanderbilt University, which is a hundred yards away. We have three small dining rooms downstairs and each one holds about twelve people. The plain decor allows the wood to be the attraction. Upstairs there are three more dining rooms and in the basement there is a bar that holds 108 people. The cooking is a mixture of corn beef and cabbage and French haute cuisine, and the chef, who has the decent Irish name of Mack McGee, is black.

We have a good location at a busy junction and I devise a newspaper advertisement which says, 'TARA is that BIG GREEN BUILDING at the junction of 21st and Broadway, behind whose walls the IRISH EXPERIENCE IS

HAPPENING … blah, blah, blah.'

Business is slow to start. Then we discover that my partner, the moneyman – a Yankee to his fingertips – is trying to enforce a 'No Jeans' dress code. Well, of course, as anyone with a bit of nous can tell you, blue jeans are one half of a business suit in Nashville. We change the dress code and word quickly spreads about the Irish experience. Within a matter of two weeks the place is full every night. On Friday and Saturday nights people are driving the four-hour trip from Atlanta, Georgia and Birmingham, Alabama, just to be part of the fun.

To say I am in my element would be an understatement. I start singing at eight thirty and do a half-hour, then two successive full hour sets, finishing with another half hour, without repeating a song all night. It is show-off heaven for me. And because most of the punters don't know what is or isn't Irish, I am making up the rules as I go along. I take great joy in teaching the crowd Irish songs and as my feel for the audience evolves, I learn that in a crisis I can always get back on track by singing 'Danny Boy' or 'Dixie'.

'I wish I was in the land of cotton …'

When I am singing 'Dixie', I often witness men being forcibly lifted into a standing position by the back of the shirt, and the perpetrators of this chauvinism are frequently lawyers and bankers who during the week come for a sober lunch or dinner, but at the weekend turn into raving rednecks. Around here the Civil War is an ongoing process and just in case anyone forgets, they wear T-shirts that bear the legend 'Hell No!'

Eventually I summon some musical help from Ireland.

The Ormonde Folk from Kilkenny come to Nashville and Eamonn, Peter and Margaret Brady and Jimmy Moore from Tullaroan are a big hit. I find me a gem of a bass player in Jake Mayer from Kentucky. I find a singing Scotsman – Jimmy Kelly from Glasgow – and later again Tommy and Jimmy Sweeney, nephews of Tommy Makem, and John Doherty from Derry use their Irish charm to tear the house down.

Over the next year and a half, the Irish Experience is the rage of Nashville. We entertain lots of country stars like Doug Kershaw and Mike Reid, movie and TV stars like Burt Reynolds and Henry Gibson and music legends like the King of Bluegrass, Bill Monroe. Burt Reynolds was a laid-back kinda guy and Henry Gibson was as small and perfectly formed as he had appeared on the famous American TV show, 'The Rowan and Martin Laugh-In'. But it was Bill Monroe who gave us the best workout.

If you remember the song 'Delta Dawn', in it the woman wore a flower and the lyric asked, 'Could it be a faded rose from days gone by?'. A faded blossom of a woman – a bit of a Delta Dawn – has begun coming into the pub on a regular basis. She tells us that she is the daughter of the great Bill Monroe. Clad in ankle-length dresses and elbow-length gloves, she behaves like a shell-shocked refugee from *Gone With The Wind*; a deserted woman, destined to live out the fantasy that she is the daughter of a bluegrass legend. And then one night she lands in with her daddy – Bill Monroe!

I have no option but to invite Bill on stage, where myself, Tommy and Jimmy Sweeney and John Doherty are flaking away at 'The Rollicking Boys Around Tandaragee'. I give Bill an introduction worthy of his reputation and then ask, 'What would you like to sing?'

'"Blue Moon" in D,' sez Bill.

I look at the three Derry stalwarts and there isn't even the tiniest glimmer of recognition in their faces. As for me, I think he is referring to the Fats Domino song of the same name, but before we get a chance to confer, Bill launches into 'Blue Moon of Kentucky', one of the all-time great bluegrass songs. When I hear the first notes, I recognize it. I shout the chords at the lads and away we go ... until that MOMENT.

It is the fashion in bluegrass for the singer to sing his verses and then step back from the mike to allow the fiddle player or some other instrument to take a solo. Bill steps back and in that moment four Irish guys look at each other and the whites of our eyes roll up in our heads, like contestants in an Al Jolsen lookalike contest. We intimidate John Doherty into stepping forward with his fiddle and from somewhere deep inside him, John claws a solo that is befitting the song. On stage, Bill is beaming with pleasure, and down at a table near the front, his fey daughter is wearing the beatific smile of someone who has been vindicated.

But on life's rollercoaster, just when you think you know all the loops in the ride, everything changes. My business partner screws me over on a personal family matter. There is no going back. I announce my intention to leave on New Year's Eve and as word gets around, we start into an ignoble, slow decline. The food and the service get sloppier. Mr Yankee gets too clever for his own good and begins cutting corners. When he starts doing the cooking himself, that's the signal for goodbye.

Looking back, one thing I am sure of is that Tara was a white experience. It was not uncommon to have a black waiter with a full tray of food pass me on the stairs singing, 'I've been a wild rover for many's a year ...' but that was as far as it went. When the dining room closed for the night, the black waiters would come down to the bar for one drink, and even though they could sing snatches of songs and had come to the enjoyable conclusion that Irish people are mad, they never seemed to connect strongly enough with the rhythms to make them want to stay. It seemed like they were moving to a different beat. And the point was hammered home forcefully the night Superfly paid a visit.

From the stage in the bar, I can see the bottom four steps on the stairs, so that the legs appear before the head. It is a reasonably quiet Tuesday night. I notice two pairs of legs in flash suits descending the stairs. Two supercool black guys enter and peel off left and right of the door, throwing a quick eye around the bar, checking everybody out. They return to the stairs and give the nod of approval. Now, two pairs of shapely female legs descend, followed by a pair of male legs in a really extravagantly flash suit, with a draped overcoat hanging behind. The bottom half of a gold walking stick is also visible.

Enter two beautiful, glamourously dressed black women. They are followed by the extravagantly besuited legs, which belong to a really cool black dude in an expensive three-piece suit, wearing shades and a stylish fedora, tilted at a rakish angle. He is carrying a gold cane with a lion's head on top. I almost expect to hear the theme from *Shaft* as they glide over to a table. One of the underlings takes the coat that is draped on the shoulders of Superfly and he sits with a woman either side of him. I am in mid-song, but I flash them a big welcoming smile. There is no reaction. They sit through a verse and a chorus before Superfly gives some sort of invisible signal and, like the tide, they flow back out as quickly as they have come in. I feel truly white.

We do eventually cultivate a few black customers, who return again and again. One of them is a newsreader from Channel 5 called Bill Perkins. We make him the first black King of Tara. On Monday nights we have a good scam going to boost business. We pick celebrities, politicians and media people and crown them King of Tara, with a phony crown, a phony sceptre and a phony Proclamation which reads: 'As King of Tara, I promise to uphold the rights of the people of Ireland ...blah, blah blah.' We offer the King and his Queen a free dinner and leave it to them to hustle their friends and family into being present for the coronation. It is a win-win situation. Egos get massaged. Tables get filled.

One night we are crowning a State Senator called Leon Perry. He is a little guy, with a moustache and a ton of arrogance. He is pretty drunk when we finally get to the coronation, but it is when he gets to the stage in the proceedings where he is starting to read his proclamation that things begin to go wrong.

I have a guest guitar player, Danny Towland, on stage for the night. Danny is playing a nylon string guitar and while Leon is rabbiting on, someone sends Danny a drink called a Flaming Hurricane, which, as you might expect from the name, has a flame on top. Danny attempts to blow the flame out gently, but only succeeds in blowing it onto his guitar. The nylon strings go boing! Danny's guitar is now on fire. He panics, and as he tries to put down the flaming guitar, he spills some of the flaming liquid onto the stage. Now the stage is on fire and Danny is manfully trying to stamp out the flames. Now his shoe is ablaze. I jump in with my boots and instantly my feet are on fire as well. The crowd is unsure what to do. But, luckily for us, in the audience is a quick-thinking friend of ours – Rick Brown. He grabs his overcoat, dashes to the stage and manages to smother the flames.

And through all the commotion, the fire and the panic, the new King of Tara, Leon Perry, hasn't paused for breath, skipped a beat or noticed a thing, '… and furthermore as King of Tara …'

We all have a good laugh and down at the bar I run into one of my neighbours, Dick Burtani, an Italian-American who is fond of wisecracking.

'Hey, Shay,' he says, deadpan, 'Is the cabaret always this good?'

Chapter 8

HAIL GLORIOUS
ST PATRICK'S DAY

St Patrick's Day in America can be a cloying experience, a bit like being overpowered by the perfume of your favourite aunt as she clasps you to her bosom on her annual visit. Patience, good humour and an infusion of strong drink help to ameliorate the worst effects of the over-enthusiasm, and I should know. Between 1970 and 1980, I played every year in different places in America, and by going with the green flow, I never had less than a good time.

My most beguiling St Patrick's Day by far was 1974 in Nashville, Tennessee, when I was running Tara. From the outset, the democrats decided that Tara, being Irish, would be unofficial headquarters of the Democratic Party. One of our regulars was the State Treasurer, Tom Wiseman. A gentleman to his fingertips, Tom was running for governor and nothing would do him but to have me accompany him to Erin, Tennessee, for their annual *Erin Go Brágh* celebrations, which included a St Patrick's Day parade.

The town of Erin, about fifty miles west of Nashville, calls itself 'a little bit of Ireland in Tennessee'. The railroad workers of the late nineteenth century felt the surrounding countryside reminded them of home, so they gave the town its name. Tom told me the nearest Catholic church to Erin was now eighteen miles away, which kind of indicated a dilution of the original Irish – and presumably Catholic – strain. I wasn't sure what to expect as Tom, myself, my five-year-old son Oisín and the pilot took off in a four-seater plane. But I was taking no chances and had decked myself out in an exceedingly loud Kelly-green jacket. And Oisín was my comfort blanket, something to hold if it all proved too stressful.

A vintage open-topped limousine, with great big fins at the back, awaited us at the airstrip. We climbed aboard and drove in to Erin to join the parade. And what a sight it was to behold! At the head of the parade was a donkey and cart, followed by a few prancing kids with banners held aloft. But the band was the clincher. The band was the local Freemason combo, know as The Shriners Band. For their owns reasons, at some point in their history, Shriners all over America adopted the fez as their unlikely headgear of choice, so everywhere I looked I saw another Tommy Cooper lookalike.

The band had taken the middle-Eastern influence a little further and were kitted out for the day in their ceremonial marching band gear: turbans, spangly waistcoats over shirts with billowing sleeves, balloon pants and slippers with turned-up toes. St Patrick and the Forty Thieves had taken to the streets of Erin. Not alone that, they were playing several varieties of middle-eastern wind instruments, which made listening to the strains of 'O'Donnell Abú' as bizarre a cross-cultural experience as a body could wish for.

Our limo tucked in behind the band and eventually the shortest parade I had ever seen, or been part of, moved off in a cavalcade of one. As we drove up and then back down the main street of the town, Tom Wiseman and myself basked in the glory and saluted the crowd with the kind of presidential wave I will forever associate with John F Kennedy. I hoped John F was looking down on us, seeing that I was doing my best for the party, and when Tom Wiseman subsequently lost the election for governor, deep inside I felt just the smallest twinge of guilt that maybe I hadn't waved hard enough.

But in all my time in America, St Patrick's Day 1977 was the doozy of them all. I was staying with my friend Bill Carson in Holliston, Massachusetts. Greed was the order of the day, and when I was offered three different gigs I didn't hesitate for a moment before accepting them all. My instinct was good. There are very few days in the life of an itinerant musician where you can say that you've had a brilliant day. On this day, the gods decided to march in my personal parade.

I was singing in Providence College, Rhode Island, on 16 March, so my St Patrick's Day began with a forty-mile drive to Suffolk Downs Racecourse on the outskirts of Boston. My riding instructions were to set up under the stand at 11am and sing for the punters as they came in to the racecourse. My mike was hooked into the racecourse public address system, so I anticipated the dubious pleasure of hearing myself, with a slight delay on the vocal. What the heck, it would be a challenge.

Facing into the unknown is part of the buzz of showbusiness, but getting the first word out of your mouth is sometimes a great feat. I settled on 'The Bould O'Donoghue' as my opening song and as I waited for that divine moment when some mysterious force within me would trigger the start of the song, I shifted from foot to foot, checking my tuning for the fiftieth time, adjusting the height of the mike for the hundredth time. And then, in an orgasmic climax to this nervous ritual, I heard the sound of my own voice ringing out across the racecourse:

Well here I am from Paddy's land
ECHO: Well here I am from Paddy's land
A land of high renown ...

The delay on the public address was murder, but I was off and running now. I swept through thirty minutes of song, stopping judiciously while a race was in progress, for fear I might startle the fillies in full flight. Apart from a few quizzical looks, there was no reaction to my singing, one way or another, but my confidence was high that I could handle a further thirty minutes with ease. Until the secretary of the course arrived.

'We'd like you to play in the Press Box, up in the stand.'

'Sure,' replied. 'But what about mikes and things?'

'Aw, you won't need a mike.'

The alarm bells started ringing as he led me to the stand.

We ascended a couple of flights of stairs and there it was, over the door, a sign saying Press Box. He pushed open the door to reveal a room about twice the size of an airplane toilet. Three hard-bitten racing hacks turned to see what the disturbance was. I was formally introduced as 'Mr Haley from Ireland' and then he stepped out and I stepped in, slung my guitar around my neck and launched into 'The Irish Rover'.

> *On the fourth of July eighteen hundred and six*
> *We set sail from the Coal Quay of Cork,*
> *We were sailing away with a cargo of bricks,*
> *For the grand City Hall in New York ...*

There was no such thing as resorting to the old showbiz trick of picking a point in infinity and singing to it. We were nose to nose, eyeball to eyeball. I knew, and the hacks knew, that we would just have to soldier on until I had satisfied the man who was paying the money. At least there was no echo. I did a bit of patter and tried to sound unhurried as I rattled through two more songs. When I finished, I bowed, shook hands with my three new intimate friends and thanked them for letting me share their space.

I went back and sang for a further half-hour under the stand. After the constrictions of the Press Box, it was a pleasure to be back *al fresco*. Nobody complained about my singing and pretty soon I was my way with a couple of hundred dollars in my fist.

Next stop was the Mayor's Lunch in the town of Everett on the North Shore of Boston at 1.30pm. I navigated the freeway around Boston and arrived with about two minutes to spare. There was no time to be nervous, and as I ladled on the blarney with a very heavy hand, the well-heeled audience were charmed 'to be sure' and in my pocket for the next forty minutes. Thunderous applause and another two hundred dollars. Thank you, yer Honor.

Easy picking so far. My next stop was a further forty-mile drive away in Nashua, New Hampshire. I was about to drive through my third state of the Union in one day, bringing blarney and bullshit in exchange for greenbacks. But what did I care? I was high as a kite on the applause of the citizens of Everett and the drive was a doddle.

The Lamplighter in Nashua is a well-known Irish pub and not alone was it stuffed to the rafters, but the adjoining dining room was also bunged to the gills. My fellow entertainer for the day was a bearded Irish singer friend of mine, Liam Maguire. We tossed and I got the pub for my first set. The punters looked up at me on the small stage with eager, scrubbed faces. It was 4pm and they were ready to party.

'Good afternoon. Y'know the way the legend goes that the three leaves of the shamrock stand for the Father, The Son and The Holy Ghost? Well, that's just plain wrong. They stand for sex, drugs and rock 'n' roll ... let's do it.'

I lit the match and tossed it onto the petrol of their emotions and we sang and shouted for a rollicking forty minutes. It was heady stuff for the ego and as I met Liam Maguire for our twenty-minute break before we swapped rooms, I was totally gorged on applause.

'How was the bar?' asked Liam.

'Great,' I smiled. 'And the dining room?'

'They're a bit stuffy,' he moaned.

The audience in the dining room looked very well dressed and groomed and were polite in their welcome. I skipped the bit about sex, drugs and rock 'n' roll on the basis that they might be a bit stuffy. But where did my pal Liam Maguire get that notion from? I sang and talked for forty minutes and this supposedly 'stuffy' audience hung on my every word, laughed at my every joke and joined in on every chorus. They were putty in my hands. In all my years in America I never enjoyed such unbridled enthusiasm from such a well-mannered and appreciative audience. It was like playing Carnegie Hall. 'Thank you, thank you, thank you, thank you,' I cried in gratitude. 'See you later.'

I swapped again with Liam and had another forty minutes of good fun in the bar. We took our break and then, oh joy, oh rapture, it was time to return to the best audience in the world: my admiring friends in the dining room. I pulled open the door and a rush of hot air slapped me in the face. My carefully groomed concert audience was now steaming with exuberance, hair askew, ties removed, a volatile mob baying for entertainment. I fought the panic, changed up a gear and brought the room to a new level of hysteria. I was crazed with power and could do no wrong, songs and gags tumbling out of me in a babble of blather and blarney. I ranted on like some demented, evangelical preacher, taking the crowd higher and higher. By now they were standing on chairs. Cheering. Suddenly a big Clark Gable look-alike in a tuxedo appeared beside me on the stage.

'Hey, Shay. I'm Chuck. I want to sing a song.'

'Friends,' I shouted, 'Chuck here wants to sing a song.'

That announcement was greeted with a blizzard of napkins hurled at poor Chuck. He ducked and weaved and valiantly attempted to start 'The Wild Rover'.

'I've been a wild rover for many a yea–'

The napkins gave way to heavy, rolled-up, linen tablecloths. Chuck was taking a pasting.

'We want Shay,' they chanted. And who was I to stop them? A sudden clang heralded the impact of a fork hitting the microphone stand. Then another. Then another. Then a knife! Chuck, still gamely wearing a paper-thin smile, leaned in to my ear.

'What should I do?' he earnestly enquired.

'Chuck,' sez I, 'This crowd is mine and that's it. I think you should raise one of those white tablecloths and let them know you've surrendered.'

I never went back to the bar again. Why ruin my perfect day? I stayed with my adoring mob in the dining room until two in the morning, by which time we were all wrung dry of emotion and too exhausted to sing any more. I had my first drink of the day and then, with the huge wedge of dollars from my day's takings making a comforting bulge in my trouser pocket, I packed away my guitar.

On the debit side, my throat felt like a butcher had taken to it with a meat tenderiser. But on the credit side, my ego was more bloated than a Donald Trump press release. I got into the car and drove back to Boston.

Hey, St Patrick. Thanks for the ride.

Chapter 9

SOUTHERN DOGS

Minnis Hinckle has a Southern accent so thick that, beside him, the regular Tennessee 'good ole boys' sound like elocution teachers.

Minnis, who is a stocky man in his forties, is Head of Sales at the Mohawk Milling Company in Newport, East Tennessee. I have just become Head of Promotions and Publicity so it is decided that I should accompany Minnis on a field trip to the various stores and outlets in East Tennessee and East Kentucky, which stock our products, Tube Rose Flour and Dixie Dude Dog Food.

As well as being the headquarters of the Mohawk Milling Company, Newport is also the moonshine capital of Tennessee. I am warned to be careful with moonshine. If the beads that ring the glass when you pour it break off in uneven numbers, everything is okay. If they don't, drink it at your peril.

After ten miles on the road with Minnis, I am ready to take my chances on a bottle of bad moonshine. I haven't understood a single word he has said so far and trying to guess where to nod and coo in the conversation is already wearisome.

How did I get myself into such a predicament? One

minute I am singing in a bar in Nashville and next thing I know, I am heading into redneck Hell, accompanied by a man who doesn't speak English as I know it.

The Mohawk Milling Company is owned by Ted Sluder, a soft-spoken gentleman who makes me feel very welcome. As his new Head of Promotions, I haven't really got a clue where to start. He suggested I take this trip with Minnis, which is proving to be so linguistically challenging.

For two days, Minnis takes me on a rollercoaster ride through the mountains of East Kentucky and East Tennessee. After a while, my musical ear kicks in and I start to understand the odd word here and there from Minnis. And as we get deeper into the mountains, it no longer matters, as I am lost in deep fascination. We climb steeply up undulating roads full of coal trucks, going up and coming down. This is mining territory, up around Harlan and Hazard and, as well as having a perilous traffic flow, it is not uncommon to round a bend and find half the road has slid down the side of the mountain.

Most puzzling of all are the number of individual fields on the sides of hills that are crammed full of junked cars, piled high on top of one another. There doesn't appear to be any roads that lead to these fields and yet someone, somehow, has filled them full of rusting hulks. I can't understand Minnis's explanation, so I decide to treat the junk fields with the same rigour as I interrogate the existence of God – I write them both off as a mystery.

Safely back in Nashville, I decide that I will begin by writing a jingle for Tube Rose Flour and Corn Meal, which

I will place in the numerous small radio stations in the numerous small towns. Frankly, I am looking forward to getting back up into the mountains on my own. I have seen so much that is fascinating that I am ready to do a bit of exploring.

I corral my musician friends, Jake, Danny and Tony, and we make a jingle:

Tube Rose, Tube Rose, Tube Rose, Tube Rose
Put a little flour (flower) in your life.

Ted, the bossman, loves the jingle and off I go driving into the mountains, bringing my son, Oisin, with me for company. It is dark when we reach the small coal-mining town of Hazard and I decide that we will eat first and then find somewhere to stay. We find the local greasy-spoon restaurant, but we skip the grits and turnip greens that the locals favour and instead we hungrily wolf down burgers and home fries until our bellies are full. Now to find us a place to stay.

Thinking myself smart, I consult the Yellow Pages and find the hotel that has its name most prominently displayed in heavy black type. It is called El Citadel.

'El Citadel is right up t'mountain,' the waitress tells me.

As far as I'm concerned we are already up the mountain, but I am in for a rude surprise. I take the road the waitress points out and as I get to the edge of town, we begin to corkscrew up the side of a steep mountain. It gets steeper and steeper and there is a sheer drop on either side of the road. My hands are sweating and my mouth is dry.

The night is black as the coal in the mountain and just when I think I can take no more, we round a final bend and there, amazingly, on the plateau, stands El Citadel, a plush hotel ablaze with gaudy chandeliers.

My jaw is on the floor as I approach the man at reception.

'Hi. I'd like a room for the night, please.'

'I'm sorry sir,' he replies, 'but we're full this evening.'

What does he mean, full? We are in a hotel implausibly stuck up on top of a goddamn mountain, deep in redneck country, and they are telling me the hotel is full? I look at the notice board to see if there is anything like a 'Squeal Like A Pig Society', having their annual dinner, but the few people in the lobby all look pretty normal. I take my five-year-old by the hand and turn to walk away.

The receptionist calls out after me.

'Excuse me, sir.'

I stop and turn back to him.

'I do have the Bridal Suite at one hundred and forty dollars.'

I look down at the five-year-old and smile weakly at the receptionist.

'Thanks anyway, but I think we'll give it a miss.'

This is just one of many interesting surprises that occur in the next few weeks as I return to the radio stations and stores to see if we are getting any feedback on the Tube Rose jingle. One day, outside Pikeville, I approach a log cabin store. The scene that greets me is like a Norman Rockwell cover for the *Saturday Evening Post*. Four old dudes in dungarees and an assortment of hats and baseball caps are playing dominoes on the wooden stoop just outside the door. Not one of them as much as bothers to look up as I walk up to them. There is a large turkey standing in the doorway and as I approach, the turkey fans its tail feathers, completely blocking the entrance. I am non-plussed. After what seems like an eternity, one of the old dudes rises and shoos the turkey away from the door. I thank him and enter.

The inside of the store is an amazing higgledy-piggledy sight. There is a counter along the left hand wall and shelves behind it that are piled high with boxes of nails, bales of cloth, hammers, saws, net fencing. An aisle disappears into the gloomy light at the rear. Down the centre is a double set of shelves and to the right of them another aisle. There is no one visibly in attendance. I call out 'hello'.

About six feet away from me, a woman's head pokes itself round the centre shelf unit at a height of about three feet. Immediately I think she is dwarf and that somehow I have drifted into a David Lynch movie.

'We're back he-uh, y'all,' the woman says.

Her head disappears again as I warily step towards her. The centre shelving finishes, and there in the well of the store, sitting at a blazing pot-bellied stove, are two women, one of whom looks like Olive Oyl from the Popeye cartoon, while the other looks like her granny. I wonder if I'm in a time warp. Outside, the day is warm, but they are still huddled up close to the flames. The only thing that is cool is the welcome they extend. I ask them about our products, but they've never heard of Tube Rose. I sit with them and chat about this and that, trying to ferret out as much information as I can about their lives. In return they show absolutely no interest in me at all and even my accent fails to arouse their curiosity one bit.

Driving away from the store, it occurs to me that this lack of curiosity is endemic up in the hills. No one ever seems to be bothered to ask where I come from. Perhaps, I reason, their lives are so full that they have no need of any truck with the outside world. Or maybe they are so backward they just don't care.

Then, one day, I am driving towards a small town in Kentucky, called Livingston. I pick up an old man who has his thumb out, hitching a ride. He is chatty and tells me that he was sent down the mines for the first time when he was twelve years old. He had to crawl on his belly to get to the coalface. Now he has black lung disease, which he knows is going to kill him.

'I lived in Florida for two years,' he says wistfully. 'I'd like to go back to Florida. I wouldn't mind it so much, dyin' in the sun.'

Then he makes a liar of me about the absence of curiosity.

'Where y'all frum?'

'Ireland.'

'Is it far?'

'It is.'

'How long would it take yuh to drive thar?'

My route takes me on to Booneville, population 252, a small town called after the legendary frontiersman, Daniel Boone. I find an oddball general store. The proprietor looks a lot like Colonel Sanders, but even though we're in Kentucky, there is no sign of fried chicken. The store is a medium-sized warehouse. The goods are piled high on top of small individual counters: gloves, soap, shoes, baling twine. It has everything and anything, including his own brand of dog food. I try to talk him into stocking Dixie Dude Dog Food, but he is firmly set on peddling his own product.

'Say, could y'all do a design for me ... an' maybe come up with a name?'

'Leave it with me.'

Back in Nashville I call my friend Jake Mayer, who was my bass player until I quit singing to become a flour and dog food pusher in the Kentucky mountains. Jake is a skilled artist and when I tell him I have the name, 'Ole Dan'l Dog Food', pretty soon he comes up with a design, which is a cartoon of a hound wearing a Daniel Boone coonskin hat, with the tail hanging down at the back. Jake comes with me to Booneville and after a lot of haggling, we get two hundred dollars for our trouble from the Colonel Sanders lookalike.

That is when I start getting pangs of conscience. Ted Sluder has given me the job of selling his Dixie Dude Dog

Food and here I am making gain from a rival. Ted takes me on a drive through the Smokey Mountains National Park and I get a chance to talk to him at length. Eventually I ask him where the name Dixie Dude comes from. He begins to rhapsodise over this great hound, Dixie Dude, who had been his best dog ever. I can see a certain moistness in Ted's eyes as he extols the dog's virtues. In the following days I write another jingle, this time for Dixie Dude Dog Food. It is payback for Ted for giving me a job and opening a window on a world that is both fascinating and strange.

And when I play the jingle to him, I swear I can see a lump in his throat.

Dixie Dude was a real good dog
He was a friend of mine
An' I never thought of goin' nowhere
An' leavin' the Dude behind
We shared many miles of road
Through good times and through bad
Now the Dude is gone but he'll always be
The best friend that I had ...

Now the Dude is gone but he'll always be
The best friend that I had.

Chapter 10

NO BUTTY OF MINE

My mother, Máirín Ní Shúilleabháin, was a well-known traditional singer. She won the McCall Cup for singing at the Father Matthew Feis Cheoil in 1931. Ma was also a very good actress and an indefatigible writer. All her life she clattered away on a series of battered Underwood typewriters, writing and reading her own childrens' stories on BBC radio, as well as contributing to magazines and periodicals.

My mother came from a small town called Killorglin in County Kerry. So too did a noted circus strongman, Butty Sugrue. This flimsy coincidence was my life raft as I eyed up the Duke of Wellington pub in Shepherd's Bush in London in the summer of 1976.

Every year, around 10 August, the town of Killorglin hosts an annual, primitive, almost pagan festival called Puck Fair. The festival lasts for three days: Gatherin' Day, Fair Day and Scatterin' Day. Each year a puck goat is picked out and groomed for stardom. When the time comes, the goat is captured on the mountainside and taken to the centre of town on the back of an open-topped truck. With great ceremony, the goat is crowned King Puck and from the truck he is then transferred to the top of a thirty-foot platform. Depositing the goat on top is the signal for a Bacchanalian orgy to begin below.

My earliest childhood memory, from when I was three, is of seeing a bull go into a barber's shop during Puck Fair. It wasn't surprising to find cattle in the street; during the day Puck Fair was a cattle fair, a horse fair, a hive of commerce, with stalls selling clothes, household goods and novelty items. In the early evening the streets would be sluiced down to get rid of the cow dung that had accumulated during the day, the rivulets of brown water flowing down the hill, washing away the sensible behaviour of the day in preparation for the madness to come.

The Fair attracted all manner of horse, sheep and cattle dealers, huge numbers of tinkers and lots of farmers, including bachelor farmers down from the hills for a once-a-year blow out. It goes without saying that it was not exactly a high fashion event, and farmers wearing the strangest of caps and caubeens, clutching fistfuls of the old red ten-pound notes, were much in evidence, pitting their wits against the chicanery of the three-card-trick men, as the cry went up 'Find the Lady'.

I can't tell you if seeing all this hoopla at Puck Fair turned Butty Sugrue on to showbiz, but whatever it was, when he grew up, he became a strongman with Duffy's Circus and through a series of exploits and feats of strength, he became famous and spread the reputation of Killorglin all over Britain and Ireland.

Butty was built low to the ground, with wide shoulders and a fantastic barrel chest. The picture of him I remember best was one where he is pulling a red London bus with his teeth. In the Fifties and early Sixties Butty was a huge attraction, but inevitably his strength began to wane and thus began his career as a publican, which led him to becoming the landlord of the Duke of Wellington pub, which venue is to be my platform for a week's gig.

I ascend from the Underground and walk down Shepherd's Bush until I see the pub before me. It has a typical London pub exterior: a shiny tiled front, brass door handles and ornate lettering on glass over the door. I don't know what to expect inside. All I know is that I am booked in for the week and that, in addition to my fee, I am also getting free accommodation upstairs.

I have recently returned from living in America and from a standing start I have had to try to put a career in place again. I have to gig to survive, but through some fluke, I have wound up putting several performers in touch with a female English agent who books the acts for Butty's pub. I eventually wheedle the gig for myself and assure her that no finer act will grace Butty's pub that whole summer.

As well as singing, I am also working for *Starlight,* successor to *Spotlight* magazine, so a gig in London means that I might be able to do a few extra interviews for the magazine, as well as pick up a few pounds for performing in Butty's.

But the problem with trying to force the hand of opportunity is that your normal critical faculties fail you and it was a sad day indeed when I neglected to consult any of the performers who had gone to the Duke of Wellington before me.

During my three-year sojourn in America, I had developed a great facility for entertaining an Irish-American audience with a mixture of Irish ballads, funny songs, parodies and gags. And when a show was going well, the buzz was easily a match for sex, so as well as the money, it was this terrible addiction to applause that had now brought me to Butty Sugrue's establishment.

As I start across the green of Shepherd's Bush, an ominous feeling of dread comes over me. I clutch the handle of my sturdy Ovation guitar case, finding comfort in its sensuous bulging shape and its solid heaviness, my anchor in this sea of impending terror. I push open the door of the bar. A few lone drinkers are hunched over pints of Guinness in a typical London oak bar, no gloss, no ornamentation, with the sun slanting through the window giving the pub a kind of unearned sexy glow.

'Is Mr Sugrue here?' I enquire timorously of the young barman.

'He's out at the moment, but he'll be back in a couple of hours.'

'Do you know anything about a room for me? I'm singing here tonight.'

'Oh yeah,' the young fella says. 'C'mon, I'll take you up.'

He comes round the bar and I follow him to a stairway that leads to a small corridor on the first floor. He isn't much good at the small talk and the ensuing silence only accentuates my awareness that everything about the place is crying out for a bit of attention and a lick of paint. He opens the door and shows me my room. The 'room' would have been perfect for Padre Pio or Matt Talbot or one of those saints who practiced mortification of the flesh, but for a broke middle-class boy from Dublin it is Spartan to a fault. An institutional blanket on a very plain bed, a one-bar gas fire and badly worn linoleum flooring are the only fuzzy, physical details that I remember of the cell that was to be my London pad for a week.

The young barman skedaddles and I close the door and sit on the bed for a while, wondering how I am going to cope. It is still only mid- to late afternoon and I decide that I would be better in the company of strangers on the street than on my own in my salubrious accommodation. I get up and open the door. A ferocious, snarling Alsatian, gums stripped back from his teeth, lunges at me from the corridor. Somehow I get the door closed and keep out the monster, but my heart is thumping and my legs have turned to jelly. My only comfort is that the dog is making such a racket that I am sure someone will come and sort everything out.

But when your tide is out, your tide is really out. No one comes to save me. And so, for the next three hours I remain a prisoner, stuck with only a dog for company and a little voice that pecks away at my frontal lobe, saying, 'Told ya so ... told ya so'.

My memory refuses to yield up a recollection of how I passed the time until I finally meet the great Butty Sugrue, but when at last I do, he glowers at me like I am someone about to present him with a bill. As I introduce myself, I delude myself that he will soften. Kerrymen are friendly by inclination and as soon as I tell him the extraordinary coincidence of himself and my mother both coming from

Killorglin, surely he will clasp me to his bosom. Butty receives the information with cold, unflinching eyes and for all its significance, I might as well have told him that my mother was a sheep herder on the slopes of the Russian Steppes.

He tells me that I will do my first spot at 9pm and that when I am finished, a car will pick me up to take me around to the 'other place'. What other place? Butty blithely informs me that after my opening set, I am obliged also to do a half-hour gig in another pub a couple of streets away. Not being in much of a position to argue, I tell Butty, 'You can depend on me'.

The performance lounge in the Duke of Wellington is big and square. The stage is very high off the ground and the 'auditorium' is sparsely populated by men only. Most of them are alone. I nervously tune my guitar. The word mustn't have got out, I think to myself as I take myself firmly by the seat of the trousers and march myself out to the microphone.

'Good evening, ladies and gentlemen. My name is Shay Healy and I come from Dublin, which is the capital of Ireland and the cultural capital of the western world.'

This is the line that knocked them dead in America. In Shepherd's Bush it goes out, hangs there for a nanosecond and drops noiselessly to the floor. There is no reaction that I can measure. They don't even have the decency to look disinterested. Some of the men stand like they are leaning on shovels. I try gags, witticisms, aphorisms, throwing the whole armoury at them, blowing some of my best material along the way. The situation is grim, and as if that isn't intimidating enough, standing off to the right, glaring at me throughout, is an unsmiling Butty, the man who shares a birthplace with my own mother and who is now radiating unhappiness through every pore of his squat, muscled body. Where is my mother when I need her?

Three men are waiting for me as I slink off stage to the sound of my own flop sweat. It is a like a bad scene from a mafia film. Why do they need three guys? Do they think I am going to make a run for it? Or are they going to skip the next gig and just beat the crap out of me for not coming up to Butty's expectations? We drive in silence for about five minutes and then they escort me into a small, packed lounge. The punters are jammed very close together and the stage, in the midst of them all, is a small, four-foot square island, one foot high. It is dangerously close to playing in-the-round and I think to myself, if it doesn't look and sound too great from the front, what's it going to be like from the back?

Because of the congestion, I have to disturb every table in my path on my way to the stage. But, unlike the Duke of Wellington, at least half the audience here are women and surely some of them will have compassion. When I get to my island, I fix the mike in position, plug in my guitar and, brave as a lion, I begin …

'Good evening, ladies and gentlemen, my name is Shay Healy and I'm from Dubl–'

The line dies in my throat. I can see from their expressions that they don't give a damn where I am from. I scan the crowd for friendly faces, but there are none. Gamely I fight through thirty minutes of the comedy equivalent of

Omaha Beach, blood and guts everywhere, until, bloodied but unbowed, I bid them goodnight to a desultory smattering of feeble applause.

The silence is excruciating as we drive back towards Shepherd's Bush and Butty's warm glow. Twice more I have to fling myself at the punters, latching on to every newcomer as a possible saviour, only to see them turn their heads away and reject me, a wretched creature, bereft of comfort, grimacing and gurning, high on a lonely stage.

As I pack my guitar into its case, I feel Butty's aura radiating behind me. I turn around and he is plonked, right there, right up against me. I am looking down at a face of a man whose expression hovers somewhere between anger and outrage. In his broadest Kerry accent he says, 'I won't be using you tomorrow night'.

Which of the two of us is the more relieved, I do not know. I retire to my room and ponder on the vagaries of gigging. Tomorrow I will have to fashion a plan to remain in London for the week. The ignominy of defeat must be kept from my peers back home at all costs. It is a night of fitful sleep, punctuated by a mocking, nightmarish echo of my own voice shouting over and over, 'Good evening ladies and gentlemen. My name is S-h-a-y … H-e-a …'

In the morning I am awake early but I stay in my room until I hear some movement downstairs. The sun is shining outside, there is no sign of my canine jailer and, ever the optimist, overnight I have put together in my head a sequence of manoeuvres that might just get me through the rest of the week as a journalist.

'Is Mr Sugrue around?'

'He'll be here in a while.'

'I'll wait so.'

When Butty finally arrives two hours later, he blanks me completely, as though I don't exist. He walks around me and almost through me, without acknowledging me at all, until eventually I pluck up the courage to walk up behind him.

'Mr Sugrue.'

He swivels and fixes me with a baleful stare.

'I know last night you said you wouldn't be using me for the rest of the week,' I stutter, 'but will you be paying me for last night?'

Two hundred pounds of muscle bristle visibly as he sticks his face up against mine and in a low, Kerry hiss, gives me the benefit of his counsel.

'Take my advice,' he says, 'and get away as quickly as you can. You're lucky to be getting out of here with your life!'

The following year, 1977, Butty died on the premises of the Duke of Wellington.

I know how he felt.

Chapter 11

NIGHTS IN BLUE SATIN

In the year of Butty Sugrue's demise I am to be found in the Butler Arms in Cavan, waiting to be introduced to the audience. I check the tuning on my guitar one more time and realise that I am nervous to the point that I can't hear whether I am in tune or not. I zip up my blue satin jacket, straighten the crease in my blue satin trousers and flex my bare toes. Yes, bare toes. For some unfathomable reason, I have decided to perform in my bare feet. If they don't like the head on me, perhaps they will like my feet? I have no explanation.

The hubbub in the lounge subsides as the emcee announces my name. One last deep breath and here we go. As I charge out into the glare of the spotlight, my whole life doesn't pass in front of my eyes. Just the three gigs that immediately preceded this one.

The first of these three gigs had happened several weeks before. I had booked the Metropole Hotel in Kilkenny, sight unseen. A friend of mine had done a gig there and lauded it to the skies. I reckoned I was easily as good an act as he was, so it would surely be a pushover for me. I dispensed a few posters to the hotel and rang a guy I knew in the *Kilkenny People* newspaper. He promised me a mention. And that was the full extent of my advertising and advance warning.

What kind of an eejit was I, at all, at all? Here I was, a grown man (if you can ever call a comedian a grown man), hoping that, in the absence of any real advertising, those punters who might like to hear me sing would pick up the vibrations from the ether and swarm in their thousands to worship at my feet.

The big day in Kilkenny arrives. I load the car, a second-hand Mini. The two big Carlsbro speakers and the Carlsbro amp take up the whole back seat, my guitar takes up the passenger seat and there is just enough room to hang up my stage shirt and trousers. I slide into the driver's seat, put on a cheerful face, bid farewell to my nearest and dearest and hear the engine give its first protesting chug of our seventy-mile journey to Kilkenny.

There is nothing quite as lonely as heading off to a gig on your own. With just yourself for company, it is easy for a chorus line of demons to come high-kicking their way into your head, but somehow, on this occasion, my innate optimistic streak takes over and I start running the coming gig in my mind, rehearsing my spiel. Already I am hearing the applause. Already I can see myself counting the money, crisp notes, rolled into a stout bundle, creating an obscene bulge in my trouser pocket.

A young lady is waiting for me at the hotel. She will collect the admission money. Together we seek out the performing room. It is bright and airy by virtue of having mirrored walls and at a guess it will hold about one hundred and fifty, which will do very nicely.

I set up the young lady at a table just inside the door of the performing room. Then I quickly lug the speakers and the amp from the car. I am so adrenalised, they are feather-light to carry. I plug in the mike and my guitar, adjust the levels, say a few test words, play a few chords and I am as ready as I'll ever be. The lighting is lacking in any subtlety, but my routine is funny and bright, so there will be no need for spotlights or mood changes. And my bright red and yellow shirt and black trousers are giving off good vibrations.

If heading off to a gig on your own is a lonely business, it is a cakewalk compared to watching the door for punters, as the hands of the clock move inexorably towards your performance time. There is no sign of anyone in the corridor outside. I walk quickly to the lobby and check the bar as well. There is no clamour, no eager knots of fans waiting for the off.

I return to the room. The young lady who is to collect the money is beginning to squirm a bit in her chair and while she squirms, I am fighting the bile of anxiety that is battling its way up my digestive tract. Nine o'clock and not a single punter in sight. She smiles weakly at me, trying to hide the pity in her eyes.

'We'll give it ten more minutes.'

We wait. It feels like ten hours. The jig is up. It is time to throw in the towel. There are no punters here now. There won't be any punters here later. I thrust a tenner into the young lady's hand and apologise for wasting her time. It is bad enough that I am embarrassed, but now she is mortified as well. She tries to hand me back the money, but I am firm and off she goes into the night.

The net losses so far are ten pounds for the young lady, my petrol money and the dry cleaning bill for my shirt and trousers. Everywhere I look in the room I can see myself in the mirrors. A thousand reflections shriek back at me, 'Fool, Fool.'

A lesser man might have crumbled and surrendered to tears, but this was nothing more than a temporary setback as far as I was concerned. The next gig would be a killer. I closed the door of the room and ascended to the stage. I turned on the power and slung my guitar around my neck. I had come this far and set up all this gear. The least I might do is sing one song for posterity. I launched into a lively version of 'When Your Belly Starts Hanging Out Over Your Belt' and my reflections smiled back at me. And even if I say so myself, I thought I sounded pretty good.

A couple of weeks passed. The gigs had been few and far between, including one gig as a DJ at a disco in Portlaoise Mental Hospital. Yet again not one single punter had shown up. But I could reason my way out of that one. The patients had surely wanted to come, but the staff in their ignorance hadn't realised what a tonic I would be for their charges. Better than all the tranquillisers in the world.

So much for being a DJ. Give me a live audience every time. Except in Monaghan. It is Sunday night in a Monaghan hotel and the law says that all bars must close at ten o'clock. But Irish publicans are never ones to miss a trick, so what happens is that the ballroom is opened to accommodate the punters, who will otherwise be turfed out on to the street. At midnight, when we are technically into Monday, the bar can then reopen. And to kill the waiting time until the bar reopens, the cabaret act does their stint in the ballroom. Tonight, as the cabaret, it is my turn to nail myself to the cross.

The women never bother to show up until midnight, when the band comes on and the dancing begins, so it is an all-male, impatient audience that stands around the walls of the ballroom, glowering in my direction as though I am solely responsible for the lack of drink. In an attempt to get closer to this surly bunch, I set up my mike about twenty yards in front of the stage, in the middle of the ballroom floor and launch off into my patter, my parodies and my jokes. For all the reaction I am getting, I might as well be back in the hotel in Kilkenny singing to no punters. But I slog on. I have another thirty minutes of this martyrdom to go, and no one can ever call me a quitter.

Then I see him, setting off from the back of the dancehall, heading in my direction. He walks with purpose. As he draws closer, I can see that he is wearing the waistcoat and pants of a well-cut suit. His crisp white shirt, with double cuffs held together by fancy cufflinks, gives him a kind of clean-cut authority. His tie is knotted neatly, his hair looks well cut and his shoes are highly polished. My intuition tells me that this is a man who enjoys the subtlety of my barbed jokes, my clever parodies and my witty asides, and that seeing me skewered on the spear of indifference has moved him to come and commiserate with me.

Now he is just yards away from me. I am like a

mongoose transfixed by a cobra. His face is impassive, but the urgency in his step is still apparent. I am in mid-song and I expect him, at any moment, to hold fast at some point until the song is finished, so that we can then share a few consoling words. But no. He keeps on coming. Now he is standing beside me at the mike. Now he leans into my ear. And now, with all the authority of a professional music critic, he speaks in a thick Monaghan accent.

'YOU'RE FUCKIN' BRUTAL!'

Brutal or not, here I am now, in the Butler Arms, the memories of Kilkenny, Portlaoise and Monaghan behind me as, barefoot, I run towards the mike, which is in the middle of the small dance floor. And when I reach the mike, I suddenly feel it – a cold, wet sensation around my bare feet. I glance down. I am standing in a puddle of beer. It is squelching between my toes, making dark stains on the bottoms of my lovely satin trousers.

Had I been wearing boots, my heart would have been in them. Instead, a great sadness suffused my body. I knew at that moment that my time as a solo entertainer in Ireland was truly at an end. Too much suffering would leave me damaged beyond repair and this was my line in the sand, my Rubicon of beer. I struggled through my half-hour and got a creditable draw with the punters, but the stuffing had been knocked out of me. I had become the washed-up boxer I had always feared I might, taking unnecessary punishment for negligible reward. All that was waiting for me down the road were further beatings and possible brain damage.

I drove home in silence, too scarified to talk, even to

myself. The blessed lights of Dublin swam into focus not a minute too soon. The need to be home had never been greater. I unloaded my speakers and my amp and stashed them away in the yard. Maybe, I told myself, I could sell the speakers.

But not my guitar. I never said I wouldn't sing again.

Chapter 12

WHAT'S ANOTHER YEAR?

And then, when the tide seemed too far out even for a decent paddle, my ship came in.

It was a cold December night in 1975. I was on the Number 8 bus travelling between Dun Laoghaire, a small town on the east coast about eight miles from Dublin, and Cross Avenue, Booterstown, which was my home, three miles closer to the city. In the seat in front were two young lads of about nineteen and as they chatted to one another, I heard the remark, 'What's another year?'

Songwriters are weirdos. We spend our time hearing possible lines of songs in the things people say. I got off the bus, turned up my collar and put my head down into the cold wind. The phrase had snagged my songwriter's brain and my creative juices began flowing:

I've been waiting such a long time
Reaching out for you but you're not here ...

'What's Another Year' had begun to write itself.

... and I've been waking such a long time
Reaching out for you but you aren't near ...

Right: My First Communion Day, 1950

Below: Abbey actors *(from left)*: Mary Craig, Eric Gorman, my father, Seamus Healy, FJ McCormick, Ria Mooney and Denis O'Dea

Above: New recruits, RTÉ, 1963 (Shay circled)

Left: Behind the camera, with Bishop Fulton Sheehan

Above: Wedding Day, 1967 *(from left)*: Ronnie Drew, Shay and Dymphna, the Pecker Dunne

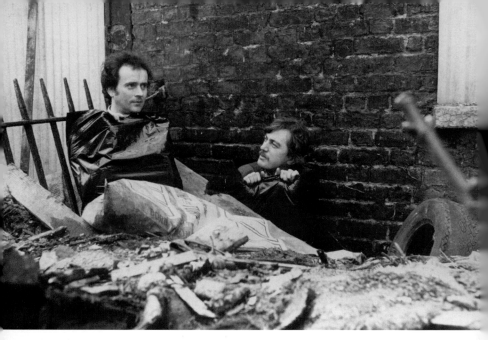

Above: Publicity shot for 'Rubbish', with Dave Pennefather, now of Universal Records

Below: Douze Points: Johnny Logan and Shay celebrate winning the Eurovision Song Contest, 1980

Above: The moment of ecstasy – The Hague, 1980
Below: Eurovision homecoming. Oisín, Shay, Fionan and Seamus Snr.

Left: Shay and Linda Martin at the Castlebar Song Contest, 1984

Above: On stage at Tara: Shay, Peter and Eamon Brady, movie actor Jimmy Hampton and Jake Mayer

Right: With Marianne Faithfull

Above: On 'Hullabaloo' with Marian
Richardson and Paschal and Tom

Left: Star Spangled Singer– my ill-fated
satin gigging outfit

I suddenly realised that this was a song about loss, about how my Da had dealt with the death of my mother in 1969, which had left him so lost and so lonely. The words continued to tumble out, and by the time I reached home, I had written and memorised four verses.

It took four more years to finish the song. Finally in 1979, I re-engaged with the song and wrote the middle-eight – the bit in the middle, sometimes called the turn:

> *What's another year*
> *For someone who's lost everything that he owns*
> *And what's another year*
> *For someone who's getting used to being alone ...*

My good friend Jim O'Neill, at that time one of RTÉ's biggest radio stars, played piano and sang the demo for me in Lombard Studios in Westland Row. The late John Brady and Noel Bridgeman from the Brush Sheils Band played bass and drums respectively, and guitarist Pat Farrell from blues band, The Business, completed the line-up. It was recorded as a nice medium-tempo, countryish ballad, but crucially, the long, high note at the finish was Jim O'Neill's idea. And that's what I entered for the Irish National Song Contest in 1980.

I was walking towards the scene dock in RTÉ in March 1980, when I heard a shriek from my friend, Carolyn Fisher, 'Your song – it's through to the Final'. My heart skipped a beat. This bit of positive news was coming at the back-end of a long, slow, meandering curve that had begun with my return from America in November 1975.

Now that I had the song, I needed a singer. At the Castlebar Song Contest in October 1979, I had met Sean Sherrard, also known as Johnny Logan. We had clicked immediately, but he nearly lost me as a friend when I took a lift with him on his way back to Dublin. The road from Castlebar wasn't the greatest and I think we skipped a few towns along the way. Johnny knew the meaning of full throttle and I made a promise to myself that, unless it was absolutely, critically, life-or-death essential, I would avoid getting into a car with him ever again.

Johnny agreed to sing 'What's Another Year' in the National Song Contest and my next call – to arranger and producer Bill Whelan – was easily the most crucial of the lot. Bill, a dacent Limerick man, is now feted worldwide as the composer of the phenomenal 'Riverdance', but back then he was working as a writer/arranger/producer. We had worked together here and there and become good friends. His talent was apparent in everything he touched. Even back then, Bill already had a musical signature, a snap he put into the music, which made it resonate with style and class.

I asked him to arrange 'What's Another Year' and his memorable score lifted the song out of its marshmallowy, country lethargy and made it into a sophisticated, evergreen, classy ballad.

Bill infused the song with a musical richness that combined the dynamics of drama and pathos. Starting with the haunting sax intro, the first two verses simply set up the story:

I've been waiting such a long time
Looking out for you
But you aren't here
What's another year ...

And I've been waking such a long time
Reaching out for you
But you aren't near
What's another year

Then came the middle-eight first time through:

What's another year
To someone who's lost everything that he owns
And what's another year
To someone who's getting used to being alone ...

The third verse brought the song to its first plateau:

I've been praying
Such a long time
It's the only way to hide the fear
What's another year

From this platform, a memorable, soaring, stark, painful saxophone solo lifted the drama higher and higher, and then, in yet another shift of dynamics, the tone dropped back down to a wistful, painful middle-eight second time through, with the track stripped of almost everything except Johnny's voice and piano:

What's another year
To someone who's lost everything that he owns
And what's another year
To someone who's getting used to being alone ...

Then a big drum fill, DUH DUH DUD DUH DUH, took us into a soaring, achingly sad last verse:

I've been crying
Such a long time
With such a lot of pain in every tear
What's another year

And now we were into the famous high-note finish:

What's Another Yeeeeeeeeeeeear

Johnny held that impossibly high, long note over a repeat line from the three backing vocalists:

To someone who is getting used to being alone.

The saxophone solo fell into the lap of a young Scottish musician, Colin Tully. He had the right look and the right sound. The three backing singers, Anne Bushnell, Pat Reilly and Rita Madigan, were all solid professionals, vastly experienced, reliable and great craic. As well as rendering impeccable harmonies, their presence was strong and reassuring for Johnny Logan. We had all the ingredients of a hit. I prayed to my muse.

When Johnny sang the song in the National Song Contest it sounded great, but I was numb, insensate and unable to discern what was good or bad in the seven other finalists. The early voting was indecisive, but then the Wexford jury gave us a maximum ten and from there the tide turned and we skated home. I rang McGowan's off-license in Carysfort Avenue and they delivered booze to our gate lodge in Booterstown. We partied till dawn, but remarkably I deliberately didn't get drunk. Some little voice in my head said, try and savour the moment so that it can be fuel for your brain in moments of doubt in the future.

In the middle of all this, my Da was in St Vincent's Hospital recovering from a stroke. Next day, the papers were clamouring for pictures of the two of us together. He was so excited we were all afraid he would have a second attack. In his day, Da, Séamus óH-Eailí, had won his own share of headlines. He was a fine athlete, who had been a Connacht 440-yards champion. During the 1930s he was a member of the Abbey Theatre and after that he joined the famous company of Micheál Mac Liammóir and Hilton Edwards at the Gate Theatre. My father also had the distinction of being the first Irishman to record an album of Gaelic poetry, and the first President of Ireland, Douglas Hyde, who wrote poetry under the pen name of 'An Craoibhin Aoibhinn' always requested that my father should be the one to read his poetry on the radio. I had been *his* son. Now he was *my* Da. He greeted this turn-around with a raising of an eyebrow and a good-humoured, sardonic snort.

Between the National Song Contest and the Eurovision itself, we put together a package. We came up with a logo of an eye and a tear, and Willie Finney, a graphic artist in RTÉ, turned it into a wonderful design, which we used on press releases, photographs, T-shirts and sweatshirts. I had a special sweatshirt made for me with the legend on the back: 'It is imperative that I win this contest'. It was a good gag. It was also the truth.

We set off for The Hague, Holland, on Tuesday, 15 April 1980. We were bivouacked at the Hotel Bel Air and we got in early and established that our hotel was party central. All the singers and musicians from the other countries would come to our hotel every night. And every night, Andy O'Callaghan, who was the piano player in Johnny Logan's band at that time, displayed his astonishing eclectic musical knowledge, as well as stamina that went beyond heroic.

We sang all night, every night, until Friday, the night before the contest, when we all grew more silent and pensive as the long, slow wind-up began. I can't remember what time I hit the bed, but knowing myself as I do, I am sure that as I lay on my pillow I was concocting great winning scenarios.

As the week had progressed, I had become more confused than I had been at the National Song Contest. Every song sounded like a winner. I was particularly fearful of the Italian entry. The singer was really cool. But late in the week I heard a rumour that his wife was threatening to jump out of a window. Idle gossip, I suspected, but consoling in its own way. Might put him off his stroke.

On Saturday, the bookies were tipping us as possible winners. I didn't really expect to win. Not for a moment. Not ever. But the die was cast. We were here for good or evil. Let the contest begin.

In a stroke of genius, Johnny Logan slipped out of the dressing room unnoticed. He made his way to the apron at the front of the stage in order to watch the people coming into the massive Halle De Congress. He reasoned that if he had a picture of what the punters looked like in his head, he would not be scared of them when his time came to sing.

Apart from writing the song, my biggest contribution to the evening was to caution Johnny to remain still and composed until he hit the last verse. His performance was impeccable. He stayed sitting on his stool and kept his composure until it was time to let the song take over. Colin Tully played out of his skin and Noel Kelehan wrung all the emotion that was in Bill Whelan's score from the orchestra. It couldn't have been better. Now it was a lottery.

During the contest, I was seated about halfway up the banked seats of the auditorium in the Halle De Congress, off to the right-hand side, looking at the stage. As the voting got tighter and the glimmers of hope began to turn to flames of possibility, I was sitting next to my wife Dymphna, scrunched in a foetal ball, softly muttering, 'Jesus, Jesus, Jesus'.

A shot of Johnny Logan holding three fingers aloft on a big screen told us that we only needed three more points to win. Three more!

And then we were there. The votes were in. We had won.

WE HAD WON!

I jumped up, arms outstretched in victory. My old friend Roy Esmonde captured the moment with his customary photographic flair. For an instant I was King Of The World.

Looking back on that moment, I have always had one regret. From where we were sitting, a long balustrade, about a metre wide, swept all the way down to the stage. Had I had enough panache, I should have parked my backside on the balustrade and slid all the way down to the stage, à la Fred Astaire. Instead, I danced down the steps to the stage, looking to hug Johnny and the girls. Alas, they had cut recesses into the stage floor, into which monitors could be wedged, and I walked straight into one of these holes. In front of all of Europe I stumbled to four faults for Ireland.

Johnny looked across at me as I recovered from my stumble and I could see in his eyes a quiet satisfaction. He had done his job and nothing would ever be the same for either of us from that moment on.

As soon as the presentation was finished, Johnny sang a reprise of the song and, showing a great instinct for memorable lines, he finished with a stage whisper, 'Ireland, I love you'. It was a moment of high emotion.

And then the television transmission was over, the lights dimmed and bedlam broke loose. An oil slick of journalists and photographers attached itself to Johnny. I realised quite quickly that there was nobody clamouring for me except an RTÉ producer, Róisín Lorigan. I followed her to the top of the theatre and did a live interview on RTÉ radio.

When I came back down, everybody was gone. I rang Bill Whelan, who was working in Windmill Lane studios, recording Planxty. We had a good laugh down the phone. As I was talking to him, Brian Masterson, the studio engineer who had recorded 'What's Another Year', arrived with a bottle of champagne. Bill told me later that the cork got stuck in the neck of the bottle and eventually they had to get a Black & Decker drill to release the flow of the celebratory nectar.

Meanwhile, back in the Halle De Congress, the next fifteen minutes are as eerie an interlude as I ever experienced. I wander through the great halls and every now and then, two corridors to the left, or two corridors to the right, I see Johnny Logan gliding past with the swarm in pursuit. I try several times to catch up, but it is futile. I meet no one I know and, despite my highly recognisable stripey blazer, my chocolate-brown straw boater, my yellow trousers, my yellow shirt and my sand-coloured beach shoes, nobody hails me as the guy whose song has just scooped the prize. Like an invisible man, I wander from room to room in a spaced-out trance.

Earlier in the day, we had been told that if Johnny won, there would be a party in a hotel about five hundred metres away. At least I would have an identity at the party. I leave the hall and set off walking in a light drizzle through an empty plaza, my perambulation becoming a ramble through Nirvana as a warm feeling of contentment permeates my whole being. I am at one with the universe.

Suddenly my reverie is broken by the sound of a friendly voice. RTÉ television's broadcasters Pat Kenny and the late Áine O'Connor materialise before my eyes. As old pals, we hug and we dance a little jig. And then we sit down on the kerb and laugh at the absurdity of it all. The improbable is now the reality. I bid them a temporary farewell and continue my journey to the victory party in the hotel.

I think I remember getting a fairly perfunctory kind of reception at the party as well. Johnny isn't with me, and without him I am just a bit of a nuisance to be tolerated rather than feted. I leave them to it and as I exit, I spot the name slot outside the door of the victory suite. In the slot is Johnny Logan's name, and thoughtlessly and uncaringly dropped on the corridor floor are the names of the three unsuccessful artists who are sharing the CBS label with Johnny.

There is no glory in losing.

Much like the aftermath of the National Song Contest, even though I stay up all night, I don't get drunk. My separation from the victory parade in the hall has given me a curious sense of detachment and disconnection. It is like I have an impenetrable shell around me and all the back slaps and the hugs seemed to be happening outside of me in an echo, far, far away. Try as they might, nobody on the outside can really imagine how I am feeling inside. I know by looking at Johnny that he is going through the same experience. I am an island and so is he, quietly incredulous that we have won and knowing that whatever else might happen, our lives will never be the same again.

The hysteria surrounding Johnny is so powerful as to be almost frightening. What I do know is that we are brothers-in-arms now and forever, our bond of friendship forged in the white-hot crucible of the Eurovision Song Contest. We have shared an extraordinary experience that no one can ever take away from us.

The word from home is brilliant. Da and my two sons, Oisin and Fionan are down in the family home in Sandymount with my sisters, Moya and Orla. Da has found the contest almost unbearable to watch, but in the moment of victory, the two boys have piled out onto Wilfield Road shouting, 'Daddy's won, Daddy's won'. My Da's excited neighbours converge on the house from every direction. And all along the rows of houses, people can be heard cheering our great victory.

And then my Da and my Uncle Tom head down to O'Reilly's pub in Sandymount for a celebratory pint. As Da puts his head around the door, the whole pub rises and gives him a five-minute standing ovation!

The homecoming is postponed until Monday to allow time to arrange a major celebration. On the Sunday evening, the Irish Ambassador throws a reception for us. I get absolutely hammered and sink slowly into a fit of drunken, maudlin sentimentality. I cry, I laugh. Then I storm off in a huff at some imagined slight. My brother Finn follows me and together we sit in a small, quiet bar and hug each other and put the world to rights. Finn is so caught up in the emotion of the moment that he insists on buying a teddy bear, which is sitting up beside a light behind the counter. The following morning, in the cold light of day, the teddy bear looks tired and moth-eaten and sports a large scorch mark on his buttock from leaning up against a naked bulb.

Later that day at Schipol Airport in Amsterdam, crazed by the thought of handsome royalties, I go mad in the duty-free shop, buying radios with in-built, three-inch television screens and other cutting-edge gizmos. Suddenly, over the airport intercom we hear a final call for passengers Shay and Dymphna Healy. The two of us set off at a gallop, bags flying behind us, and we are making good progress until Dymphna runs smack into a plate glass window. She reels back, an ugly gash spouting blood. We keep on running and scramble on board with not a second to spare. The hostesses patch up Dymphna's cut and then they get back to the important job of pouring champagne for a plane full of happy people.

As we begin our descent into Dublin, my brother leans forward and tugs my sleeve. As I turn, he smiles at me and says, 'I wish the merry-go-round didn't have to stop'.

A massive crowd is waiting, thronging the balcony and the Arrivals area. Da is there with Oisin and Fionan by his side. On the tarmac a swirl of managers, gardaí and family mill up and down. Every time Johnny waves, the crowd swoons. Every time I wave, they merely wave back.

We hold a packed press conference and then someone whispers, 'There's a limo waiting for you out back.' The limo speeds us to our first stop, Madigan's in Donnybrook, our local pub. When I walk in, the entire place erupts in applause. It is a really touching moment that stays with me still.

The next stop is St Vincent's Hospital, where Dymphna gets a couple of stitches in her wound. When we finally arrive home, the local kids in Booterstown had slung a sheet on the wall outside the house. On it is scrawled 'Congratulations and Welcome Home'.

The limo is back for us that night to take us to the victory party at the Country Club Hotel in Portmarnock. The joint is rocking and it is nice to connect with all our show-biz friends. But what I remember most is the big screen. Back then, a big screen was a big deal. But it isn't so much the screen that impresses me as much as what is being shown on it. On the Friday night before the song contest, RTÉ had shown one of the most famous episodes of the American soap 'Dallas', in which the baddie, J R Ewing, had been shot by a mystery assailant, triggering wild speculation as to the culprit. And so, all night long on the big screen they show, in rotation, Johnny Logan winning the Eurovision Song Contest ... followed by J R Ewing being shot in 'Dallas'.

I never discovered the genius responsible for the choice of programme, but I take my hat off to him or her. Here was a person who understood instinctively what the rest of us were struggling to put into words. The Eurovision Song Contest is nothing more than a soap opera with songs!

Chapter 13

THAT'S INCREDIBLE

The songwriter must forever be alert to opportunity, so when the elevator doors open to reveal the words 'Marvel Comics' above a lifesize figure of Spiderman clambering up a wall, I step from the lift without hesitation. To hell with the book publisher who is expecting me in an office on the 11th Floor.

'Hi,' I greet the receptionist in my best Americanese.

'Hi,' she says back. 'Can I help you?'

'I would like to talk to whoever looks after the affairs of the Incredible Hulk.'

She doesn't bat an eyelid. 'The woman who looks after that is out right now. She won't be back until about three.'

'I'll come back,' I tell her. And then just as I turn to leave, I spot the box of Incredible Hulk headed notepaper.

'Would you mind if I took a couple of sheets of that?'

'Not at all,' she says obligingly.

She hands me six sheets of paper, which have my pal the Hulk, clad in purple pants, emblazoned on the top. I hurry back to my apartment and quickly go to work with a pen, drawing a huge clump of shamrock in the Hulk's giant hand. It looks as good as I had visualised it might.

My travelling companion in America is John Stephen-son, a young Turk of the Irish arts scene. His uncle has given us the keys to his Park Avenue apartment, and from this swanky base anything seems possible. Even talking Marvel Comics into letting the Incredible Hulk become a comic symbol of St Patrick's Day!

We aren't in New York to do business. In fact we are on a mission to see the Rolling Stones in San Francisco; one of the Guinness clan is leaving tickets for us at the gate. For me, aged thirty-eight, the trip is supposed to be a belated, uncomplicated, hedonistic, American, rock 'n' roll odys-sey. Until the Hulk goes and sticks his nose above the parapet.

When John sees the drawing of the Hulk clutching the shamrock, he begins to laugh. 'What are you up to now?'

It is time to explain. I tell him that about a year ago I had written a song for the comedian Brendan Grace, called 'The Reason Why The Incredible Hulk Is Green' and with a bit of enterprise I reckoned it could become a huge Irish-American hit. The chorus goes:

Oh me father and mother were Irish
They came from Skibbereen
And that's the simple reason why
The Incredible Hulk is green
Yeah that's the simple reason why
The Incredible Hulk is green ...

The truth is, I am a lifelong funny song junkie. I've been clean for a good stretch, but the Hulk song heralds a serious relapse. My propensity for funny songs goes back to when I realised that I wasn't a good singer, so I swapped being a singer for being a funny guy instead.

Now it's three o'clock and I'm back in Marvel Comics reception.

'Hi. Remember me?'

There is good news: the woman who looks after the Incredible Hulk is back. I tell the receptionist what a wonderful guy I am; how I'm a famous, successful songwriter and how I have this great idea for the Hulk.

She relays my self-aggrandising information to the woman who looks after the Hulk and, remarkably for America, where it is always a struggle to get through the blockers, this woman agrees to see me. When I get into her office, she lets me rant until I am up to high doh. When she senses I've stopped, she tells me that my idea is very interesting, but that I am in the wrong place. The music for the Incredible Hulk is handled by MCA Records in Los Angeles. 'Ring,' she says. 'Ask for Richard Silliman.'

And then something even stranger happens. I ring, ask for Richard Silliman, and by some miracle I get straight through to him. No blockers. As I launch into my leprechaun spiel and outline my idea for the Hulk, I can hear Richard Silliman chuckling on the other end of the phone. He is charmed by the wheeze and when I outline my travel plans, he tells me to get a tape to him in Los Angeles and to ring him when I get to San Francisco.

The chase is on. I ring Irene Keogh, the manager of Windmill Lane Studios in Dublin, where I had recorded the song. I ask Irene to Fed-Ex the tape to Richard Silliman and while 'The Incredible Hulk' is winging his way to MCA headquarters in Universal City in Los Angeles, we are winging our way to San Francisco for a date with the Rolling Stones.

Ours digs in San Francisco is the swankiest hotel in town, which sits on top of Nob Hill. The room costs an arm and a leg and we have an up-close view of the second hotel block, which is situated about three feet from our window. We make a call to our ticket contact, who is staying in the same hotel. She invites us across to her room for a drink. We go downstairs and cross the lobby to the other block. When we reach our contact's room, the door opens to reveal a floor-to-ceiling window with a panoramic view over San Francisco. It is a firm reminder that in the global scheme of things, we are little more than peasants. Back in our own room, we have the view we deserve.

The next day is sunny and warm, with cloud-free blue skies. We take a cab from Nob Hill to Candlestick Park, about a fifteen-minute ride. The big bowl of a stadium is home to the San Francisco Giants baseball team. The place is buzzing when we get there and I am elated to actually feel the excitement I had hoped for. The day is perfect. The setting is perfect. And we have tickets waiting for us at the gate. Don't we?

We traipse from gate to gate, but nobody seems to know anything about our tickets. The Moonies of music are handling security. They stare past us, eyes focused on infinity, repeating over and over the dismissive mantra, 'Have a nice day'.

Calamity. The Rolling Stones will be on stage at any

minute and we are still outside the stadium. We make a dash around to the rear and there, outside a gate with heavy security, are two women sitting at a table. They know nothing about our tickets either and they are about to blank us when myself and John go into a duet of woe that would bring tears to a rolling stone.

'We've come five thousand miles to be here,' we chorus. 'FIVE THOUSAND MILES.' They look at one another and simultaneously crack a smile. Our pathetic, doe-eyed duet has worked and as we become the owners of two precious backstage passes, the Rolling Stones sweep by us into the stadium in two very small vans. Inside, we stand awestruck, thirty feet from Mick Jagger, as he does his warm-up high kicks and contortions out of sight of the audience. And then the music starts and we rush around the front to see the Dark Prince of Rock 'n' Roll come prancing on stage.

We are living our dream. Our passes work miracles as we gradually make our way out front. Silver-tongued John spoofs us into the Press Box, which is right at the top of the stadium. Drinks in hand, we watch this phantasmagoria climax in a finale of exploding fireworks and the release of thousands of huge black balloons. Helicopters are buzzing like angry bees above the stadium, swooping in over the roof and then buzzing back out again. High above, the vapour trail of a passenger jet prescribes a circle as the pilot gives his passengers a birds-eye view of the show below. All my senses are sated.

We find a busy bar and decide to wait until the crowd has dispersed. I leave the bar and go back into the stadium for one last look. The artifical turf looks like a battlefield, littered with the detritus of the departed army. And standing forlornly, almost at midfield, is a small pup tent, still erect. It has done its job and now it is the last reminder of a glorious rock 'n' roll day that has lived up to everything it promised.

Next day, I have a sore head, but it is soon forgotten. It is time to ring Richard Silliman. 'We're heading south today and we'll be staying in San Simeon overnight, so we expect to be in LA in mid-afternoon,' I tell him. Just saying LA feels so cool. I'm talking to someone in LA about *my* song. I'm hot. Everything is falling into place. Destiny has taken over.

'Ring me tomorrow when you arrive. I've set you up to meet someone from our Record Division at three thirty. His name is Bill Straw. And he says he knows you.'

Gasp! He knows me! Bill Straw knows me! My reputation has gone before me. An executive at MCA knows me. Surely this is another omen.

Driving down Highway I, I get my first full glimpse of the Pacific Ocean. My pulse has quickened; colours seem more vivid. Fields full of pumpkins that stretch in rows for hundreds of yards, present a unique picture of America in the fall. We pass by the legendary Big Sur. We pass the redwood forests. Can it *get* any better?

After an exhilarating drive down the sinuous cliff-top highway, we arrive in San Simeon, which is situated half-way down the west coast, about four hundred miles from LA. San Simeon is home to Hearst Castle, the famous art deco mansion of media mogul William Randolph Hearst.

We stay the night and join the hundreds of dull tourists who are also staying in the mid-price motels that line the highway on either side for a hundred yards or so. By ten o'clock, everywhere is quiet. No buzzing bars, no music. Reading the phenomenal scores on the machines in a games arcade gives a clue to what people do for kicks around here. We retire early and sleep doesn't come easy. Bill Straw knows me!

The 7.30am tour of Hearst Castle is enjoyable, but I am finding it hard to concentrate. Once we get moving, I drive fast, with great purpose, and soon the road signs above my head read 'Los Angeles straight ahead'. Finding Universal Studio City is no problem. Fate is at the helm and the directions unfold with ease. We park the car and my muse is dancing with delight as I announce myself to the receptionist.

Richard Silliman is a handsome man in a suit. He is warm and generous in his response to the lyrics of the song, even though he has yet to hear it. He is very encouraging as he leads me along to Bill Straw's office. We knock and Bill opens his door. He is also a pleasant-looking man, I guess somewhere in his mid-forties. He has fair hair and a kind face. He makes me welcome and gives me a Coke. Richard Silliman excuses himself and now here we are, just the three of us. Bill Straw. Destiny. And me.

'Richard says you know me.'

'Yeah,' says Bill. 'I met you at the Castlebar Song Contest. I had a song in the final.'

He has had an entry in an obscure song contest in the remote town of Castlebar in the far west of Ireland! Is that it? Is that the extent to which he knows me? Big deal! This is not the pedigree I had anticipated for the man who is going to introduce me to the American music industry and fill my coffers with greenbacks.

'I really love your song,' says Bill, 'But ...'

But? But what?

'... but the Hulk has been cancelled by the network, so the merchandising is all going to S-L-O-W D-O-W-N.'

Bill's speech has slowed down. I'm slowing down. My rollercoaster ride is grinding to a halt and resentment is waiting for me at the terminus. I become aware that Bill's office is windowless and oppressive. I think to myself, what would he know? He is just a battery hen, in his cubicle, alongside all the other hens in their identical cubicles. A man with a head full of straw and feet of clay.

I stumble out the front door, deflated and dejected. It takes me hours and several vodkas before I get a grip back on reality. And when the spell is finally broken, I begin to grin at the absurdity of the quest that is now in tatters. It is only a year since I won the Eurovision Song Contest and sold a million records with a classic mid-tempo ballad. For the first time in my life, I'm being taken seriously as a songwriter and yet here I am on the far side of the world, trying to convince a major record corporation that the Incredible Hulk with a bunch of shamrock clutched in his hand can be the next big thing! It is just so *me*, you wouldn't believe it.

Bill Straw is forgiven. It's not his fault that the Incredible Hulk TV show has been cancelled. I take back my petty insults about his office and his job. I soften to the point where I hope that the next time he enters a song in the Castlebar Song Contest, he will be victorious.

A couple of days after I get home to Dublin, Richard Silliman writes me a lovely letter.

Dear Shea,

I am returning the cassette of your very enjoyable version of the Incredible Hulk … I think it is very cute, but I do not know what other avenues to pursue here with respect to commercial exploitation of it …. If you have not talked to Alice Donenfeld about this, perhaps you would forward a tape to her for her consideration.

Best of Luck,
Yours very Truly,
Rich.

Alice Donenfeld will have a long wait. I dust the song off every St Patrick's Day and sing it wherever I happen to be, if they let me. And that's as far as it goes.

Someone called the cops they came and took us off to jail
And there inside the prison cell everyone looked pale
All except our friend the Hulk, whose face was turning mean
He roared, 'This is incredible' and turned Forty Shades of Green
He pulled the bars from out the walls and threw them on the floor
We all escaped and spent the evening Hulking Out some more:

Oh me father and mother were Irish
They came from Skibbereen
And that's the simple reason why
The Incredible Hulk is green
Yeah, that's the simple reason why
The Incredible Hulk is green.

Chapter 14

UNDER THE KOCH

New York is a networking kind of town. You meet somebody; they give you a business card and pass you on to
someone else. Before you know it, it's like that game 'Six
Degrees of Kevin Bacon', where in six moves you can connect to almost anybody on Earth. For instance, I want to
connect to Hollywood producer George Lucas. I know
Andrew Kavanagh, who was a writing partner of Philip
Lee in Dublin and Philip is now working on George
Lucas's ranch. That was easy, wasn't it? Two moves and I'm
in George Lucas's ear.

But networking is not always good for your health. For
instance, on one of my many American forays, I landed in
New York in January 1986 and one week later, through a
lightning series of 'connections', I am standing with a
guitar around my neck in the kitchen of Gracie Mansion,
home of Hizzoner the Mayor of New York, Ed Koch. Also
present are the Mayor's chef, his secret service bodyguard
and his extremely large dog, Archie, who looks like an
Irish wolfhound with a haircut.

Gracie Mansion is on the fashionable Upper East Side of
New York and I have to pass through two sets of sentries

to make it into the house. I am met by the chef, who brings me upstairs to his kitchen. It is a fine big kitchen and the chef offers me food, but I am too apprehensive even to think about eating.

The Mayor of New York is a very powerful man. It is a hands-on job in the 'city that never sleeps'. New York is the hub of the universe and Ed Koch has a very strong profile as a man of action, absolutely confident and competent in running *his* city. Political power in America is almost obscene in the way it reduces grown men and women to craven obsequiousness. They really fawn on their elected representatives and I could only speculate on the number of people who would cheerfully knife me to be in my place tonight, close enough to touch the hem of Hizzoner's coat, never mind being about to entertain him.

Of course, as well as being a political powerhouse, Mayor Koch also likes to think of himself as a sophisticate, someone who appreciates the arts. A variety of big names, from Judy Collins to Pavarotti, have performed for the Mayor in the very drawing room that is about to be my stage. This is a big honour and a major coup for the boy from Sandymount, Dublin 4.

The chef tells me that tonight the Mayor is entertaining a group of twelve people. All the information I can get about my audience is that they are 'wearing suits'. On learning this, I am sort of wishing that I could be in a suit myself. But I'm not. I'm in a very tight black jacket over an open-necked white shirt. My trousers are black pantaloons and I have shoes that would have no trouble doubling as slippers. On top of all that, my blonde hair-dye job has started to turn an alarming shade of orange and I have it cut into a short and spiky, all-action, trendy haircut. For all the world, I look like a demented head waiter from a gay vegetarian restaurant in the East Village.

My contact has advised me to do a couple of my 'funny' songs, but little is she to know that in the past, in matters of choosing suitable material, I have sometimes been reckless rather than prudent. Flying in the face of the on-the-ground intelligence, I determine to proceed with the repertoire I have fixed in my brain.

The Mayor comes into the kitchen. Ed Koch is bigger than he appears from his pictures. He scarcely makes eye contact with me as he shakes my hand in a cold, perfunctory manner and informs me that he will be calling me in a few minutes. Then he is gone and I'm alone again with my nerves and the bodyguard. As I respond to the Mayor's beckoning finger, the bodyguard says, 'Don't worry man. It'll be a breeze'.

The drawing room is furnished in 'auld decency' style. The furniture is a cluster of big armchairs and couches, rich and comfortable, like the people seated on them. The gender divide is about half and half and all the men are over sixty and cut from the finest patrician mould. They look a scary bunch of cold bastards. The women are demure, but expensively dressed. There is one woman about my own age, an attractive blonde. She is the only one who greets my entry with a half-smile.

I try to look them all in the eye, but they are too busy perching on the edges of their chairs and sofas. Hizzoner intones my list of credits: 'Well known in Ireland ... won the Eurovision Song Contest ...' which he extravagantly and erroneously describes as the Irish equivalent of The Grammys ... blah, blah, blah. The blank faces tell me all I need to know. Grammy schammy.

Now it's my turn to blah blah. 'Good evening. My name is ...'

Normally in such circumstances an Irish accent commands a certain kind of curiosity. In this case there is not a flicker of reaction. I feel like a small Irish insect on a petri dish, waiting to be dissected by some non-Irish etymologist.

But instead of sprinting for the door as a sensible man might have done, I find myself introducing 'West Cork, West Cork', a parody of the New York anthem 'New York, New York'. At least they'll know the original. 'This is a song of emigration in reverse,' I tell them.

Start spreading manure
And making the hay,
I'll drive my ass and cart to it
West Cork, West Cork ...

As I hit the final verse, stony faces look at me as though I am a piece of turd on their shoes.

We'll be living on food
The vegetarian way,
I'll grow some beans and fart in it
In old West Cork.
And if the craic's not there,

I'll just move on to Clare,
It's up to you
West Cork West ... dah, dah, dih, dah.
Dah, dah, dah, dih Wessssssttt Coorrrrkkk.

The applause is as quiet and delicate as the closing of butterfly wings. I take a deep breath and introduce a cute Irish song, 'Nancy Hogan's Goose'. It is a story whose charm would melt the hardest of hearts: the tale of a philandering gander, who having enjoyed congress with Nancy's loose goose, finds himself in the dock. The judge dismisses the case with a caution to the gander that he stay away from the goose and in the last verse the gander sings,

Oh, when I go down to O'Grady's store
I'll feed meself on oats and grass
And I'll court Nancy Hogan's goose
When Nancy Hogan is gone to Mass.

They are not amused. More butterfly wings. The good-looking blonde woman catches my eye for a brief second. In that brief contact I can feel her saying to me, 'You're fucked and there is nothing I can do to help you'.

Inspired by her empathy, I launch into my final song, yet another parody, and explain that this time it is a parody of Lou Reed's 'Walk On The Wild Side', except that it's about the Irish living on New York's East Side. Now, a parody is a fine thing if people know the original, but from the blank expressions, it is blatantly obvious that there is no Lou Reed album to be found in the record collections of these upright citizens. The point of it is completely eluding them. But does that stop me? Not a bit.

Kathleen she was such a silly girl
She got caught up in the social whirl,
Now her Irish eyes are shining bright
'Cos she's pushing coke up her nose all night
She says toot ... toot ... tooraloora on the East Side ...

At this point, just as I'm getting into my stride on the song, the drawing room door bursts open and Archie the hound comes bounding into the room, his clumsy body galumphing all over the snobocracy of New York. He turns his attention to me and rears up on his hind legs and whacks me and the guitar a resounding blow, managing in the process to play a passable chord in tune. Hizzoner bustles him out of the room and as the discommoded guests adjust their suits and dresses, I go for broke with my final verse:

Mike and Pat were working pretty hard
Said Mike to Pat, 'Hey let's go avant garde
I can hiccup and you can fart
We'll tell them that it's performance art
Hey babe, take a walk on the East Side.

They clap out of nervousness, unsure of what new calamity is waiting to befall them. I bow and exit to the kitchen.

'Jaysus, Jaysus, Jaysus, Jaysus, Jaysus. Fuck. Fuck. Fuck.'

'Whatsamatter?' the bodyguard sez.

'That,' I tell him with trembling voice, 'was the most humiliating experience of my life.'

'Aw, c'mon. It wasn't that bad.'

'No,' sez I. 'It was worse than that.'

'At least they clapped.'

'So?'

'Pavarotti was here. They didn't clap.'

So I did better than Pavarotti. So what? It is no consolation to me. I can still feel the cold sweat in my armpits and my fingers are trembling. I pack my guitar, my dignity shrieking at me to get out of this place as quickly as possible. I bid the bodyguard goodnight, and just as I reach the door he calls out after me.

'Hey! The dog ... he never did that for anybody before. The dog really liked ya!'

Chapter 15

WHERE THE HELL
IS JOE PAPP?

Joe Papp, the famous Broadway producer, is dead. And whilst I wouldn't wish this condition on Joe, at least I know where he is. Which is more than I did in the spring of 1986, when Joe went missing and left me up on a tightrope for a nailbiting, agonising, heartbreaking, nervejangling three weeks.

My fortieth birthday present from my wife was the ultimate synthesiser of its day, a Juno 60. It was an inspirational gift and within a week I had written a space-age rock opera called *The Knowledge*, which stretched to eighteen songs and all the recitative in between.

The plot is simple and aimed at a family audience. In a joint effort by the major world powers, three ten-year-old kids are launched into space to see if they can find a civilisation that might teach us how to slow down the awful arms race and stop Armageddon.

The show was staged by two youth groups, in Dundalk and Sligo, but apart from that, after two years of pitching it to record companies, movie producers, theatre producers, cartoon animators and amateur musical societies, I was still stuck on the launch pad, in my rocket. When I had started out, the project had been fuelled by the years of plenty in the wake of winning the Eurovision Song Contest. Now the pinch had hit and with a small fistful of dollars and a big handful of high-level contacts, I set off for New York to prove the doubters wrong.

The BIG song in *The Knowledge* is 'Edge of the Universe'. This is my baseball bat for knocking down doors in the Big Apple. Courtesy of an introduction by Paul McGuinness, my first call is to Michael Leon, who is 'the man' in A & M Records. He is slim, good-looking and stylish, dressed in an expensive suit and tie. His wavy, grey hair hangs to his shoulders and he sports a roguish gold earring. He would have made a handsome pirate.

Michael's office is on the 32nd Floor. It is one of those coveted corner offices, so mandatory in a business whose central philosophy is one-upmanship. The view over Manhattan is magnificent and today it is further enhanced by falling snow. I feel like I am in a movie.

My pitching routine is straightforward. I play 'Edge of The Universe' and if they like it, I hit them with the spiel. The hardest part is listening to the song. I can't look at Michael while it is playing, so instead, I look at the ceiling and the shapes of the lights. Three times I read the instructions on the fire extinguisher on the wall. I try to read the album sleeves on his desk, upside down. I memorise the posters on the wall. And then the track is finished. Michael likes it. He also generously offers to make half a dozen copies of the script for me and he wants to hear the full demo of the entire musical.

I dance out of his office, flushed with optimism, and head for Mary Ellen Benannotti at Chappel/Intersong Music Publishers. She thinks 'The Edge of the Universe' is 'very pretty'. She makes a copy of the tape for herself and, like Michael before her, she offers to make me copies of the script. This is too easy.

When I had set out earlier, I hadn't expected the snow to get heavier, so I am wearing inadequate, soft, black leather shoes. No matter. I am on a roll and weatherproof. That is, until I arrive at RCA to meet Wendy Goldstein.

Oh Gawd! Wendy is tough, New York, Jewish and acidly negative.

'We'd have to get a million-dollar marketing budget from a major movie company, or a Broadway producer, or something like that. *Chess* bombed for us. I mean ... drone ... drone ... drone.'

I don't get to do my spiel. Instead, Wendy insists on playing me Barry Manilow's new single. Barry Fucking Manilow!

'The kids are the only ones that are buying records,' she drones. 'Now, I know they don't buy Barry Manilow, but if there is a good track and they can dance to it in their rooms, y'know?'

As a matter of fact, I don't know. Barry's new single is a travesty and so is my meeting with Wendy. When I step back out onto the sidewalk, the slush goes straight through my shoes and as I trudge to the subway, utterly deflated, I glumly see that I don't have the winning lottery numbers.

Wendy has put a hex on me. Over the next three days I pitch to four more record companies, but they are all negative. I am painfully aware now that I am in for the long haul and that means having to find a job that will allow me the flexibility to keep appointments. A small ad in *The Village Voice* newspaper and blind intuition lead me to the New York City Ballet, which is on 64th Street on the posh Upper West Side. They are looking for telemarketers. James Jackson greets me and explains that they have a campaign, selling subscriptions to the ballet. The work starts at four in the afternoon and finishes at nine. Perfect.

My first taste of telemarketing is unnerving. The room has ten booths, five down each side. James Jackson sits at a table at the top of the room, a bit like a teacher. His job is to keep us motivated, so there are bonuses of five-dollar bills for big sales and he also keeps a steady supply of chocolate chip cookies flowing.

The nine other telemarketers are reasonably experienced. They are out-of-work actors, singers and writers, so while I am comfortable in their company, I am also a little shy and nervous. James hands me a sheaf of tear sheets from a computer printout. It is a list of telephone numbers in the New York and New Jersey areas. I decide to listen for a while before I try my first call and the more I hear, the more I am freaked. Nine people, with nine different routines create a scary cacophony.

A big Jewish girl called Nancy opens with the same line each time. 'Hi, Mrs Schwartz, am I disturbing your dinner?' Noel, a Sephardic Lebanese Jew, is much more aggressive: 'Well, don't come cryin' to me if you miss out.' And every time a phone rings, gay Michael shouts out in his campest voice, 'I'll get it.' And we laugh, every time.

I scan the list and let my eyes fall on Mrs Murphy in New Jersey. Surely my accent will snag her and I'll be a hero in jig time. Mrs Murphy answers the phone and I switch on to autobabble.

'Hello, Mrs Murphy. My name is Seamus and I'm a leprechaun from Ireland who is offering you the crock of gold of a subscription to the New York City Ballet ... yada ... yada ... yada.'

Mrs Murphy lets me finish and then she says, 'Seamus, gimme a break. I'm packin'.'

As well as making my debut selling ballet subscriptions, I am also gigging for the first time tonight for a great warrior, Stevie Duggan, one-time hero of the Cavan Gaelic football team. Stevie is the manager of Paddy Reilly's Bar at 28th and 2nd. By 10.30 there is not a sinner in the bar and I am nervous.

'I'll start singing, Stevie. See if the noise will attract them in.'

It's an old ploy, but it works. I'm hardly finished my first song when four punters arrive. Then two more. Then another couple. There is now a respectable crowd and my gig goes down so well that almost everybody stays until 1.30. At 2am I go back on stage to perform for a motley crew of one Arab, four Irish lads, two Americans – one fat, one skinny – a girl who fancies me and her boyfriend who doesn't, a lone black man and a Mexican who keeps shouting at me, 'I liiiiike youooo ... hee is good ... heee is very good ... youuuu sing good ... I like youuuuu ...'

Days slip away between working at the ballet and gigging. I am waiting for three record companies to call me back about *The Knowledge* and when I try to force the pace, I come up against very efficient blockers. I am becoming frustrated and my very next appointment confirms that the pressure is getting to me.

Lisa Judson at CBS Video is friendly and welcoming. She lets me do my pitch and then she tells me that although she is not the right person for the project, she will send on the script and the tape to the proper person for me.

'But can I give you one bit of advice?' she asks.

'Sure.'

'Don't pitch it yourself.'

'Why not?'

'You're bleeding all over my carpet.'

She is too right. My bloodstains are all over Manhattan. I recount my story to Geraldine McInerney, the PR representative of Billy Joel and his wife, Christie Brinkley. I had interviewed her a couple of weeks previously for a magazine about her stint as the first editor of *Image* Magazine in Dublin and I had told her all about *The Knowledge*. She had suggested that she bring it to mega movie producer, George Lucas, so I drop her a tape and a script. Two days later she rings me and tells me that it gives her 'goosebumps'. She hears it the way I do. Now I know I'm not mad.

'Forget about George Lucas,' she says. 'I have some very powerful friends, including the Broadway producer Joe Papp, who runs the Public Theatre on Lafayette Street at Astor Place. And I did the press on that hit musical, *The Mystery of Edwin Drood.*'

Joe Papp is particularly famous for his annual midsummer outdoor presentations in the theatre in Central Park. Geraldine rings me next day to tell me that she has a meeting set up with Joe Papp for the following Tuesday. We agree that she will be my agent. If nothing else, it will keep the bloodstains off Joe Papp's carpet.

Tuesday arrives, but Joe Papp doesn't. He promises to be back in touch on Thursday to reschedule the meeting. At this point I am very homesick and strung out. The gang at the New York City Ballet have become my support team and nightly they ask for an update on developments. Tonight I have nothing to tell them. And not only that, my blarney has deserted me, so I manage to sell zilch in the way of subscriptions.

It is pissing rain when I get off the subway at Astor Place. Every day and every night on my way to and from the subway, I have to pass by the Public Theatre and tonight Joe Papp's name mocks me from a huge poster in the window. I am eight blocks from home, my back hurts and my spirits are so low they mingle with the garbage that lines every block. I walk head down through the pouring rain. In New York, even the rain is an over-the-top expression of nature.

Thursday comes. The news is that Joe Papp wants another copy of the script and another tape of the show! Back I go, up on the tightrope. I am invited to a very swanky party in a brownstone on East 85th, the home of some millionaire or other. I go just to fill in time and as soon as I find myself in a mill of people, I realise I have made a bad decision.

I meet Nick, a cool guy in a silver suit, with a fantastic

mohawk of curls on top of his head. Nick wants to be a recording engineer so we talk music. Then he produces a small bottle from his pocket. He unscrews the top, which underneath the cap tapers to a tiny spoon. He reaches into the bottle and comes back with a spoonful of coke for me. And then another. The coke kicks in and as soon as it does, I know it is going the wrong way. I become completely paranoid and flee into the night, cursing Nick and Joe Papp. Things don't always go better with coke.

Joe Papp has been missing for a week now. Bruce, his PR guy, tells Geraldine that the script is doing the rounds. I am on my way to Geraldine's for dinner, when I get a call from a friend, Mary Tierney. She is very active on the art and theatre scene in New York and next week she is starting to work for, guess who? Joe Papp. She tells me that no news is good news.

When I reach Geraldine's, her news bowls me over. 'Joe Papp phoned me. He says they will make a decision on Monday and I'm to have you on stand-by for Monday evening or Tuesday morning.'

At 1am I ascend from the subway to Astor Place. I have had three vodkas and a joint. I stop outside the Public Theatre and imagine myself walking through the doors on Monday to meet Joe Papp. Then my imagination runs completely riot and I see myself in Central Park on a hot midsummer's night, standing at the back, while the crowd rises in a standing ovation for *The Knowledge*.

Monday dawns. I haven't slept well, with Joe Papp hopping in and out of all kinds of strange situations in my dreams. It suddenly occurs to me that I don't know what

Joe Papp looks like, so how the hell can he be in my dreams? Up at the ballet, one of the guys, Roger, has made a big sign, which says NO NEWS YET. He pins it on my back and says it is to save me having to answer the same question over and over. Everyone asks, 'Why are you wearing a sign on your back?'

Roger volunteers to make a sign about the sign.

It is 11pm now and I am getting no answer from Geraldine. Stay positive. Remember what Mary Tierney said. No news is good news. It must mean that Joe Papp wants to see me in the morning. I try to distract myself by watching television, but my concentration is lousy, so I pick up my guitar and bash away at it until an angry banging on the ceiling below reminds me that it is now 2am. I tell myself that in the morning the sun will come up and Joe Papp will smile on me, bright as the sunshine. And then I lie down and punch myself to sleep.

Hanging around the apartment is murder. The sound of the phone startles me. I grab the receiver.

'Hi. It's Geraldine.'

'What's the story?'

'All right. I got a phone call and Kevin Kline is opening in *Hamlet* at the Public Theatre on Friday, so everybody in Joe's organisation is in a tizzy and they tell me there won't be any word until at least Friday.'

Fucking Friday. That's three whole days away. Does Joe Papp not know the meaning of mercy? I have been in New York nine weeks today and I am celebrating by wandering aimlessly around this terrifying limbo, this tortuous valley that must be traversed in search of someone, anyone, who will like and understand my work. It is a vale that is irrigated by self-piteous tears, a hopeless hollow where dreams can turn to dust.

Does Joe Papp do this to everybody? Is this a part of the game, to soften me up? Just Joe having a power trip?

No call comes on Friday and so on Monday morning I start calling the record companies I had been to at the start of this odyssey. Michael Leon, my pirate friend at A&M, is not available till Wednesday. Geraldine rings to say that Kevin Kline's *Hamlet* has got a drubbing from the critics and Joe Papp is going missing for a couple of days. So what the hell is new, Joe? I think murderous thoughts and direct them at Kevin Kline. Asshole.

On St Patrick's Day I feel lucky and ring Michael Leon. He is in and he takes the call.

'Hey, Shay.'

'Hey, Michael. Happy St Paddy's Day. Did you have any further thoughts about *The Knowledge?*'

'Okay Shay, here's what I think. There is nothing I dislike about your musical. It would take great vision to put it together as a record project, but I think I have that vision. But what would really tip it into my basket would be the involvement of another medium. If there was a stage show, a video, or some other medium, I could be pushed.'

Where the hell is that shithead Joe Papp? He is the vital 'other medium'. I call to Geraldine's for a drink. She is celebrating St Patrick's Day and feeling no pain. She puts her finger to her lips before I bring up Joe Papp's name. I think, at that moment, I know for the first time that Joe is gone and she hasn't had the heart to tell me. I don't even bother to tell her what Michael Leon has said. I throw back my drink and head for my gig in Tramps.

Tramps is a blues club owned by Terry Dunne, a very likeable guy from Drimnagh in Dublin. He is dressed in a tweed jacket, a green shirt and a yellow scarf and he looks for all the world like John Wayne in *The Quiet Man*. I have lined up a pretty bizarre band for the night. On bass is Robin Irvine, a former member of the Irish showband, Chips, and now Cindi Lauper's tour manager. On keyboards is my Lebanese friend from the ballet, Noel Hattem. Maria on flute, Mary Rose on fiddle and Mary on harp, are all ex-Bunratty babes. The drummer, Chuck, has cried off, but who cares.

We are a raggedy-ass musical mess. The girls are very nervous at the beginning, but the gang from the ballet arrive and pretty soon the place is jumping. The gags and the songs pour out of me. I invite people up from the audience and we have a real party going. And to crown it all, rock star Stevie Winwood, who is in the club to enjoy himself, comes on stage and plays with us for an hour. The looks on the girls' faces as they drink in the awesomeness of playing with a bona fide rockstar is worth the price of admission alone.

In my role as ringmaster, I feel strangely liberated. My shoulders have relaxed, the tightness has left my forehead and I know what has happened. I have let go of Joe Papp. I know now for definite that *The Knowledge* is not going to happen. Instead, in five days time I am going to go home. I need to see my family. And I need to sleep in my own bed.

I start to strum the tune of 'If You Were The Only Girl In The World.'

'Ladies and gentlemen, I'd like to sing a special request for a friend of mine, Joe Papp.'

If you were the only guy in the world
I think I would turn you down ...

The gig is over. I jump in a cab and ask the driver to take me home via Astor Place. As we glide past the Public Theatre, I give an old fashioned two-fingered St Patrick's Day salute to my ex-friend, Joe Papp.

And now Joe Papp is dead. And I'm not.

Chapter 16

HIDING BEHIND
THE SHADES

You need three things to be a busker. A neck like a jockey's bollocks. A pair of shades. And fierce determination not to be embarrassed. I have the first two, but I am not sure if I have the third.

It may seem a bit perverse that someone who is about to sing for pennies should indulge himself with a cab to get him to his public stage, but as I slide into the back seat of the big yellow cab, there is method in my madness. I have set myself a challenge: if I can't make back my taxi fare, the exercise will be utterly redundant.

I am dressed oddly, even by New York standards. My outfit starts with a leopard skin cap, perched jauntily on top of my head. Beneath the cap is a pair of gold-framed, wrap-around sunglasses. My outer top garment is an Op-Art T-shirt I have been saving for a special occasion. The T-shirt covers a heavy black work shirt and beneath that there are two more T-shirts and a thermal vest.

When it hits you, New York cold is like a thousand micro-fine needles being plunged into your body simultaneously, so I am also wearing long johns and over them my mock-leather, skintight, rock 'n' roll trousers, two pairs of socks and my black Chinese slippers. I'm ready for action.

Fifth Avenue dead-ends into Washington Square Park, a public park with a full-scale replica of the Arc De Triomphe standing proudly at its entrance. The park is a favourite meeting place for New Yorkers and visitors alike and it is also one of the premier busking arenas in the western world.

In the centre of the square is a circular arena, a bit like a duck-pond without the water. Instead of water there are circular steps on which punters can sit, either to soak up the sunshine or to observe whoever might be performing.

Radiating outwards to the four corners of the square are four pathways and a pathway also runs around the perimeter, which is unfenced, so that you can see the moving traffic on all four sides. There are seats dotted around the park. There are also play areas and there is a massive totem pole carved from a giant tree.

The bright, harsh, midday, January sun has attracted a reasonable sprinkling of people. I scan the crowd from behind my shades and realize, to my chagrin, that I don't really have a clue how or where to start. I have rigged up a sock-like bag, which hangs down from the top of the guitar neck, but I am conscious that now that I am on the brink of making my debut as a busker, I haven't thought it through particularly well.

I stand myself off to one side, at a point where one of the pathways meets the perimeter. A woman pushing a buggy is walking towards me. I gulp in some air and burst forth:

Well I never felt more like singing the blues ...

The woman jumps back in fright and the child begins to cry. Jaysus, what a start! She circles me, never taking her eyes off me, as though I am going to pounce again and terrify her offspring once more. Eventually she slinks away and leaves me to my solitary embarrassment.

A change of tack is called for. The people are not coming to me, so I must go to the people. I climb into the central arena and walk around inside, singing to approximately twenty people who are sitting on the steps. I can see them reacting, but nobody seems to be in a hurry to give me any money. In desperation I approach a young girl who is sitting alone. Still playing, I say to her under my breath, 'Please put something in my bag, start the ball rolling.' She blinks at me uncomprehendingly. 'A dime or a cent ... start the ball rolling.' She fishes in her pocket and comes up with thirty-five cents, which she drops into my sock. We're off. A dollar here. A dollar there. A quarter here. An apologetic dime there.

When I feel I have milked them for all they're worth, I sling my guitar around behind my back and retire to a seat to count my earnings. Four dollar bills and three dollars, thirty-five cents in change. I've made the cab fare on my first outing. I am impressed with myself to say the least, but I am also conscious that this busking business is trickier than it appears.

After a while I set myself up in an area facing a row of seats. People gather.

On the Fourth of July eighteen hundred and six
We set sail from the Coal Quay of Cork ...

From behind my shades, I can see how people slither away as soon as I make any move to approach with my collection bag. My technique is flawed and despite the fact that I appear in three Japanese home videos and am the subject of every kind of camera from professional Nikons to dime-store Instamatics, I only make a total of two dollars and fifteen cents for my fifteen-minute stint.

While I am singing, a stocky, bearded Puerto Rican wino, dressed in denim jeans, denim jacket and denim cap, has been urging me on, shouting encouragement. 'Sing it to me, man.' He is drinking from a bottle wrapped in a brown paper bag.

When I finish he says, 'That was good, man.'

'Thank you,' I reply. 'But it's not very profitable.'

'Hey, man, my name is Frank. Go get yourself a cup of coffee and come back in a while. There'll be lots of people here when Tony does his thing in the middle.'

One cup of coffee and a doughnut later, I am back in the park, lighter by $3.00. Total expenses to date are $2.10 for the taxi, $3 for the coffee and doughnut. Total take so far, $9.55. I'm winning the battle, but the war doesn't look too promising.

Tony has a snappy act. He works in the duck-pond arena. The steps inside are full and the punters are three-deep the whole way around the outside. Tony does some fire-eating and some balancing tricks and in between he has a really good line in patter. Halfway through his act, he passes a fireman's helmet around the crowd, which at this stage must number close to two hundred. I watch enviously as the hat fills up with one-dollar and five-dollar bills.

I continue to observeTony until I sense him drawing to a close. I ready myself and as soon as he finishes, I let rip again. My Puerto Rican friend, Frank, reappears. He introduces his friends, a Seminole Indian called Johnny Lightning and a Cree Indian called Melvin. They start throwing rock 'n' roll shapes, so I oblige with 'Blue Suede Shoes'. Next thing you know, a tall, bald, black man in a long, tight black overcoat is bopping with us. In his right hand he carries a Bible. He sings along and then he gets so excited that he throws off his coat and begins to jitterbug like a madman. Now our whole little area of the park is having a street party, but as soon as I make a move to cash in on this free concert, the crowd melts away and I am rewarded with a measly $4.10.

Frank, the chairman of my Puerto Rican Fan Club, gives me a swig from his bottle. He swears it is brandy, but it tastes more like Buckfast Tonic Wine. The tall, bald, black man introduces himself as Pastor Emil Harris and insists on giving me his address in case I ever 'need' him.

I thank my new friends for their support and set off walking towards home on East 6th Street. The cold has wrapped its icy hand around my heart and the worst part of the anti-climax is that, at that moment, I have no one to share my experience with. I get some curious stares as I trudge along with my guitar on my back, but my good humour has leaked away with the cold and I can't be bothered smiling back.

Later that night I am singing in Paddy Reilly's Bar on 28th and 2nd Avenue. I recount my experience to a group of new friends I have made and in my usual fashion I glamourise the whole thing to the point that two ex-Bunratty girls – Mary who plays harp and Maria, who plays flute – agree that we are going to tackle Washington Square Park as a trio the very next day.

With the support of two others, I am a new man. The day is again cold and sunny and when we find the most sheltered spot, we soon draw a sizeable crowd as we play jigs and reels. And then, to our consternation, a bunch of Jesus Freaks decided to set up just yards away from us. They begin to bellow, 'Yes, I love Jesus.' and our crowd of admirers turn on them and start shouting, 'Shaddup, you assholes'. An ugly New York incident is imminent, so we decided to strike camp and move on.

Our next step is inspired. We jump on the subway and head for Grand Central Station, the capacious, magnificent edifice smack in the middle of Manhattan, with its fabulous staircases, its massive chandeliers and its giant clock. Everybody knows Grand Central, even if only from the movies, and after the cold, here in its warm bosom we happily set up and instantly attract a big crowd.

And then something extraordinary happens. A smallish man in a dark crombie coat steps forward. His clothes are expensive, his hair neatly slicked back, his grooming impeccable.

'Would you mind,' he asks, 'if I sing?'

'What do you want to sing?'

'I'd like to sing "Bonnie Annie Laurie" in the key of C.'

I look at the girls. They nod their assent and we launch into 'Bonnie Annie'. Our new busking partner trills along in a very pleasant, tuneful, light tenor voice. Our audience

Above: It's a knockout – Shay and Barry McGuigan
Below: *(from left)*: Mags Fegan, a red-headed Shay, and Chris de Burgh

Above: Philo with daughters Sarah and Kathleen

Below: With Bono and friends on the MGM special to Florida

Above: With 'Possum' George Jones

Below: A chance to warble 'Stand By Your Man' in Tammy Wynette's bath

Left: Host Shay and Joyce Ward as Rita at loggerheads on 'Nighthawks'
Above: Man with two peckers: Shay, Pecker Dunne plus marionnette
Below: With Ian Dury

Above: Friends in Low Places, with Garth Brooks

Below: Larry Cunningham, the Man from Granard

Above: With close friend Bill
Whelan, composer of 'What's Another
Year' and 'Riverdance'

Right: The strangest gift I ever got:
Volume VIII of Jack Glover's Bobbed
Wire Bible, a book about barbed wire

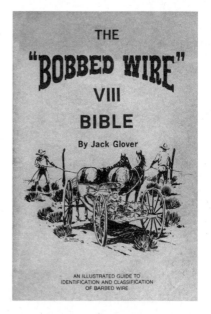

THE
"BOBBED WIRE"
VIII
BIBLE

By Jack Glover

AN ILLUSTRATED GUIDE TO
IDENTIFICATION AND CLASSIFICATION
OF BARBED WIRE

Above: Yeeehaw! Roy Rogers and cowboy Shay on a Honda 'Trigger'

Below: The Dinosaurs Club: Jim McCann, Billy Connolly, Christy Moore, Ralph Mc Tell, Ronnie Drew, Phil Coulter, Shay. *In front*: Paul Brady

is rapt with attention, right to the last note. He receives a warm round of applause and then he reaches into his pocket, produces a ten-dollar note, drops it into our basket, bows stiffly and vanishes back into the crowd.

Just then a cop appears. 'You gotta move on,' he says. 'Even though I like your music.'

'We'll finish after this one,' I whisper.

Our haul for a ten-minute spot is $26.95 and while we are in good mood, I suggest that we go the whole hog and try the subway downstairs. It is cold and draughty and we are no sooner set up then we realise it is a bad decision. We repair for coffee and a divvy up.

But even as we part, I know I am not finished with this busking lark. I had always thought that no platform existed upon which the cheap exhibitionist in me would ever be intimidated. But in busking or, as they call it in America, street performance, I have finally found a medium that inhibits me. The challenge is too much and the next day, still in my wrap-around shades, I set up in Times Square subway, where the shuttle from Grand Central arrives.

Times Square is the smelliest subway in the world. The stench of urine floats along the passageways and derelicts of all descriptions drift to and fro, looking for heat and handouts. This is the sternest test of all.

The shuttle from Grand Central arrives every seven minutes. As soon as it comes to a halt, a frenzy of passengers piles off the shuttle, heads down, hell bent on their destinations. The waiting punters board the train and it departs, creating a lull until the empty platform slowly fills up again.

Smart boy that I am, I put down my hard-shell guitar case in front of me, on what I gauge to be the main track from the train to the exit. I have seen other buskers in this exact position. I toss a dollar bill and some change into my guitar case as bait and await the riches that will soon be coming my way.

The shuttle arrives. The doors open with a whoosh and like ants the passengers pour forward towards me. It is all I can do to drag myself and my guitar case out of their path as they bustle past me with unseeing eyes. I consider myself fortunate not to have been trampled to death and for spite I resolve to persevere. I gauge that it takes a repertoire of just three songs to work this slot and as I finesse my timing, I am getting a lot more attention, even if I'm not getting any money.

A bent-over, shabbily dressed old woman shuffles up to me and hands me a dollar. 'I'm sorry I don't have any more,' she says, before shuffling away again. Her kindness keeps me going a while longer and when the next train departs and the platform is quiet I become conscious of a very tall, gangly black man starting to circle me at a distance. He stays throughout the arrival of the next set of on-rushing passengers and when they are gone, he and I are the only two people left on the platform.

He is coming towards me now and as he gets closer, I can see he is younger than I first thought. I guess he is somewhere in his late thirties and he is carrying a battered duffle bag. He has a patchy beard and he is wearing cheap denims and a well-scuffed pair of boots. His long, sad face gives me a shy, gap-toothed smile and then he reaches into his back pocket and comes up with a small object.

'Hey, man,' he says. 'I don't have anythin' of value to give you ... but I'd like to give you somethin'.'

He drops a small pocket-knife into my hand. It has a cheap and chipped imitation mother-of-pearl handle, one blade, a nail file and a tiny scissors. No sooner has he placed it into my hand, than he starts to back away. I reach out and we grip each other in the brothers' handshake.

'Thank you, man,' I tell him. 'You don't know how much I appreciate that.'

That is enough for me. I can go home now. And even though I have enjoyed my joust with the denizens of the Big Apple, I know in my heart that I will never be a proper busker until I am able to face them without the shades.

Chapter 17

PHILO – A VOICE
FROM BEYOND

The very last time I interviewed Phil Lynott, lead singer with Thin Lizzy, was in the grounds of Howth Castle in 1984. He was appearing in a video for his friends, Gay Woods and Trevor Knight, who called themselves Auto Da Fe. I grabbed him during a break in filming, turned on my small dictaphone tape recorder and we took a half-hour stroll around the grounds, by the light of the moon.

It was an upbeat interview. Everything about him was optimistic. Thin Lizzy was finished as a band, but he was confident that he had got himself back together after a sloppy period when he was rumoured to be doing a lot of drugs. He especially talked about his responsibility as a father to his two daughters, Sarah and Kathleen. I was happy to hear this confident Philo back in charge of his life.

Later I drove him into town and we went to the Pink Elephant. We were given a VIP table and soon we were lashing back champagne. But what I remember most from that night is that at regular intervals Philo would produce from his pocket an envelope full of cocaine, dip his thumb into the coke and whatever came out balanced on top of his thumbnail, he would hoover up his nose. He was discreet about it and none of the punters saw what he was doing, but it was the most coke I had ever seen and it struck me that his behaviour sharply conflicted with the sentiments he had expressed to me just hours before.

Oddly enough, through no fault of my own, I already had a drug history with Philo. A couple of years previously I had been a guest at his thirtieth birthday party in stately Castletown House in Leixlip, about fifteen miles outside Dublin. The party room was full of happening people, having a good time, when suddenly the place erupted. Detective Sergeant Dinny Mullins and his feared Drug Squad were busting Philo's party. People began running towards the windows, clawing their personal stashes of drugs from their pockets and chucking them out into the night.

Next day, the *Sunday Press* carried screaming headlines and a full report of the goings-on. One of their reporters had been at the party. Somehow or other, I was fingered as the man who had tipped off the press that a raid would take place. How anyone ever came to that conclusion I still don't know, but in the next few days I got two anonymous phone calls, telling me I was going to have my legs broken. Nothing happened and Philo never subsequently mentioned it to me, so to this day the mystery of the tip-off has never been explained satisfactorily.

The last time I saw Philo alive was that night we met at Howth Castle in 1984. Two years later, on 4 January 1986, I was in a shop on 8th Street in New York when the news came over the radio:

'British rock star Philip Lynott died today in a London hospital. He was thirty-six.'

My legs buckled for an instant. Philo wasn't supposed to die. He was our first genuine Irish, bulletproof rockstar. How could it have happened? I knew he was taking a lot of drugs, but I didn't ever think he was going to die so young. It was like he had obeyed one of those trite aphorisms of youth: 'I'd rather burn out than rust'.

As the enormity of his death sank in, I got mad on his behalf. Philo would have hated being called a British rock star. In Ireland we are accustomed to having our sportsmen and movie stars annexed by the British press when it suits them, especially when the stars in question are successful. Philo would have been apoplectic. Robbie Brennan, who played drums with Philo in one of his later bands, Grand Slam, summed him up perfectly.

'When Philip was in England, he was from Ireland. When he was in Ireland, he was from Dublin. When he was in Dublin, he was from Crumlin. And when he was in Crumlin, he was from Leighlin Road.'

As I walked the streets of New York, I couldn't stop thinking of Philo. I had interviewed him a couple of times for magazines. I'd travelled twice for *Starlight* magazine to see him on 'Top of the Pops' in London and I was accustomed to meeting him in Dublin in the Bailey, the Pink Elephant and especially in the most louche club of them all, Wilde's, the favourite hang-out of the Dublin demi-monde, where rock stars, criminals and oddball members of the gentry vied for the spotlight.

Philo was always ready for a laugh and in my experience I never saw him pull the old 'I am a rockstar' moody. And because he was so approachable, most people didn't bother him by approaching him. He was 'one of our own' and consequently he was left to his own devices.

Just how much affection he enjoyed from ordinary people was captured in a very revealing and brilliant video of one of Philip's later songs, 'Old Town', which was shot in Dublin by Gerry Gregg. In one sequence, Philo is walking up Grafton Street, Ireland's poshest shopping thoroughfare. The familiar beanpole figure with the massive Afro haircut lopes along in a tight-fitting black coat, with the collar turned up, his long spindly legs jammed into impossibly tight black drainpipe trousers, which finish in a pair of pointy-toed black cowboy boots. All heads are turned towards him and as he passes, a collective smile flickers across the faces of the punters, as though the sun has just come out again after a shower of rain.

And now they have erected a bronze statue of Philo on Harry Street, just off Grafton Street. The boy is back in town.

When Philo, Eric Bell and Brian Downey got on the boat to England to try and make a name for themselves, they serendipitously bumped into the late British DJ John Peel, who was one of the most influential arbiters of musical taste on BBC radio. He championed Thin Lizzy and they began to build a bit of a reputation. At the urging of their Irish manager, Ted Carroll, the band recorded 'Whiskey in the Jar', and in the process, Eric Bell stamped his name forever on rock music when he played one of the most brilliant and individualistic guitar intros in the history of rock.

Originally 'Whiskey in the Jar' was to be a B-side, but when they flipped the record, it became a huge hit and Thin Lizzy became famous. But the rocked-up Irish ballad became a bit of a monkey on Philo's back and for a long time it overshadowed a lot of his other songs. It wasn't until 'The Boys are Back in Town' became a worldwide anthem that Philo got his well-earned recognition as a major rock star.

In 1995 I made a documentary, 'The Rocker', which was a tenth anniversary tribute to Philo. His wife, Caroline Crowther, told me, 'Philip was a rock star even when he was brushing his teeth'.

Philo's journey to rock stardom began with a young band called The Black Eagles. Then he was taken under the wing of Brush Shiels, a musical dynamo on the nascent Dublin rock scene, who had a band called Skid Row. Brush taught him how to play the bass guitar and throw a few shapes. The tall, handsome Philo was a sensation.

At most, there were a handful of black people in Dublin in the late Sixties. Philip's father was a Brazilian seaman called William Parris, who didn't stick around when Philomena became pregnant. She made a decision, as a single mother, to bring Philip home to Crumlin, where he was raised by his grandmother and the rest of the Lynott family, while Philomena stayed working in Manchester. But she had a strong bond with Philip and made frequent trips home to be with him.

One of Philo's friends from Crumlin, Mick O'Flanagan, told me how he would sometimes bring Philo back from gigs. Mick is only about five feet tall and Philo was about six foot four. Mick had a very small Honda 50cc motorcycle and during Philo's early band days, Mick would often give him a lift home. 'Can you imagine what we must have looked like?' laughed Mick. 'This very small bloke, driving a very small bike, with this very tall black fella on the back?'

In his teens and early twenties, Philo was a bit of a joker. He would get into a taxi and spin a yarn to the driver that he was the son of an African chieftain. The way I heard it, one such journey ended with the taxi driver trying to take advantage of the 'prince's son' by overcharging him. 'Fuck you,' says Philip, as he jumps out of the taxi and legs it. The taxi driver is momentarily flummoxed. And then he gathers himself, rolls down the window and shouts after him, 'And fuck Martin Luther King'.

The biggest disappointment for all of us who admired Philo was that America never fell at his feet while he was alive. The day before the band set out to conquer America, guitarist Brian Robertson cut his hand in a fight and had to pull out of the tour. Robertson and Scott Gorham had developed a unique twin guitar sound, which, along with Philo's voice, had become the signature of Thin Lizzy. If Robertson hadn't cut his hand, who knows what might have happened?

One of the band members told me that Philo started acting up in America and as a consequence, the tour was messy. They would check into a hotel and, no sooner had they settled in than they would all have to move to another hotel, because Philo had deemed his bed to be too small.

Nobody knew it at the time, but the long, slow decline

was beginning and even though he was to have many more great gigs, the unravelling of Philo had begun. It continued until Christmas Day, 1985, when he was taken into hospital, no longer the indestructible rock star, just another sick man.

His mother, Philomena, refused to accept that he was dangerously ill.

'I said to him, "C'mon Philip, we've been through things before," and he'd always got better.'

She watched over him, helplessly, day and night, as his vital organs began to fail, one by one. Over and over Philo kept saying, 'Sorry, Ma'. He knew he had blown it and yet one of the nurses told Philo's wife Caroline that when she had noticed his lips moving, she leaned down to hear what he was saying and the dying rogue was singing 'My Way'.

On the night of 4 January 1986, still reeling from the news of Philo's death, I journeyed to an apartment on 86th Street on the Upper East Side, to tape an interview. I was using the same small dictaphone recorder that I had used to interview Philo in Howth Castle a couple of years before. After the interview, as I walked back down 86th Street to the subway, I began listening back to what I had just recorded with the woman I was interviewing. She finished her last answer and then, before I got a chance to turn off the tape machine, I heard a voice I recognised immediately:

'Now that I have two kids I'm going to be more responsible.'

It was the remnants of my interview with Philo and it seemed like he was talking to me from beyond the grave.

As I walked down the street, replaying Philo's poignant, self-deluding words, my heart was filled with a great sadness.

Chapter 18

ONCE IS ENOUGH

Monday night is one of life's great downers. In the restaurant, bar or music business, the sensible thing is to write off Monday. And it's not just in Ireland. I've walked into all kinds of places, in many different countries, only to be confronted by the ineluctable fact that when it's Monday night, it's Monday night all over the world.

But, truth be told, against such certainties I was born to kick. In the mid-Eighties, flying in the face of providence, common sense and statistics, I had a country rock band called Risque Business. Our battleground was the Coconut Grove Lounge in Stillorgan in south County Dublin and our preferred time of jousting was Monday night. And it was great fun. Except for the night the row broke out.

Sometimes we were a four-piece, sometimes more, the only constants being myself on guitar and Sean Devitt holding down the groove on drums. The numbers could go as high as eight on occasion and guitar players and bass players rotated in and out on an ad hoc basis. The songs were humourous and I did plenty of good-natured shouting at the crowd. Lots of musos used to turn up for the laugh and it was an excuse for us to play a bit of music and smoke a few joints.

We had a small but loyal following. Part of the attraction was the uncertainty of who might show up to sing. We had everybody from Eurovision legend Johnny Logan to one of Ireland's first rock stars, Jimi Slevin. When Robbie Overson was playing lead guitar, we would have a loud shirt competition, with a predictable result: Robbie always won.

The bass players, Tony Molloy, Philip Myatt and John Kearns, who all played superbly, were typically phlegmatic bass men and I could always depend on them as the set list changed for the umpteenth time. Bass players never get muscled, hustled or bustled.

The near-regular keyboard players were Eoin White and Ronan Johnson, aka 'The Milky Bar Kid'. But it was Jim O'Neill, the voice of Today FM, who was tinkling the piano and singing a few songs on the night the row broke out.

Music is such a divine joy. It fills up our senses, transports us across barriers of space and time and sometimes lifts us higher than a rainbow. And because music is such a personal transaction, the variety is infinite, so that sometimes the beauty of other peoples' choice of music can astound you.

But it can also go the other way. There are certain songs that instead of astounding me, make me grind my teeth and clench my fists. And the winner, by a long chalk, is Billy Joel's 'Piano Man'.

Now it so happens that I have had lots of laughs with 'piano men' and I find them most agreeable company. All of them, without exception, have kinks. They all play differently and they all have their distinct eccentricities. But more than that, they are the latter-day *jongleurs* of the music world.

In his song, Billy Joel does his best to ruin the image of the real piano men by telling us that, glamourous as it may look, playing and singing in a bar is as lonely as being the on-duty counsellor at the Samaritans.

Just shut up and play, Billy.

Anyway, the night the row broke out, Jim O'Neill had just launched into 'Piano Man' with my grudging permission. Suddenly we hear a voice being raised at the bar. The noise is coming from a big, handsome, heavy-set guy, with a thick but neatly trimmed moustache. He is in shirtsleeves and his shirt is expensive and open at the neck. Incantations like, 'Do it,' 'Yeah,' and 'Great song,' are getting stronger by the minute as Jim drones on through Billy's dark, dank dirge. The guy at the bar is now incandescent with joy and seems to like 'Piano Man' so much that I am quite excited to think that maybe at last I am in the same room as my polar opposite.

As the sorry saga of the sad and lonely Piano Man whimpers to a close, I notice one of the waitresses approaching the stage. She holds out a tray in front of her and there upon it, sitting up and begging to be pocketed, lies a crisp, new, £50 note. 'That man down there said this was for playing "Piano Man".'

I grab the mike and address our new admirer:

'Sir, your generosity knows no bounds and it is our pleasure to play for you.'

'Right on, man,' he shouts back.

Bejapers, he's a Yank. Or a 'Septic Tank', as they are

known in Dublin rhyming slang. I like Americans, but a Yank is the kind of worst-nightmare, loudmouth American, and this guy looks like a contender.

The sound of further kerfuffle reaches my ears and I notice that our new friend is now starting to buy drink for all his new neighbours and friends at the bar. He also seems to be tipping waitresses and bartenders for just having the good grace to exist. The bar is grinning from end to end and bonhomie and good humour are the order of the day.

Suddenly, out of nowhere, Monday has become the best night of the week and Risque Business are kickin' ass. Presently we are joined on stage by Maggie Cody, a great blues singer and a good-looking woman. Maggie is in great voice and as she belts out a twelve-bar blues, I see the tray, with a waitress on the end of it, once more approaching the stage. This time it is adorned with a fifty-dollar bill. A big, cheery wave from our man at the bar confirms that once again our benefactor is the Septic Tank.

At this stage, an atmosphere of joy has spread across the whole room. Everyone is infected by this outburst of profligacy and our loud friend is at this stage just short of lighting his cigar with a twenty-dollar bill. I pour on the charm in my spiel, lavish praise on all things American and just before we take our break, the Bill Gates of the Coconut Grove continues with his philanthropy by buying a round of drinks for the band.

We are a happy bunch of boys as we take our break, join the crush at the bar and listen to stories of unbridled largesse. I edge along until I finally meet our friend.

'Charlie,' he booms, sticking out a big paw. 'What's your name?'

'Shay.'

'Hey, Shane, you guys are just great.'

'Yeah. Well, Charlie, we think you're great, too.'

I surrender five minutes of my life and jaw aimlessly with him about absolutely nothing. Charlie is lit up like a hundred-watt bulb and the light is falling on everyone. Bartenders are giving me the thumbs-up and the waitresses are winking at me. I haven't known such popularity before or since and to tell the truth I am enjoying it. But if only I had known what was going to happen, I might not have been smiling quite so broadly.

We get back on stage and the band is cooking. I am full of 'What The Fucks' and all the better for it too. A 'What The Fuck' is a drink we invented one demented Monday. It contains one shot of vodka, one shot of kahlua and one shot of Bailey's Irish Cream and it gets its name from the conclusion that after two, the only thing left to say is, 'what the fuck'. My eyes are positively glistening with joy in the absence of pain. The band sounds better than ever.

For the third time there is kerfuffle at the bar and this time the outcome is a bottle of champagne on a tray heading for the band. The waitress comes carrying five glasses and a bottle of Dom Perignon. The good news is that it will be a four way divvy-up, as the non-drinking, non-smoking Ronan Johnson is back in the line-up on the piano. We pour the champagne to the accompaniment of whoops and hollers from the crowd and at this stage, recklessly taking the piss, I toast our friend, The Septic.

'God Bless America and top of the evenin' to ya.'

'You guys deserve it,' he announces to the bar.

Then the waitress who had brought us the champagne beckons me over to the side of the stage and hands me a note from the Yank.

The note reads: 'Play "Piano Man" again.'

And that's when the row breaks out.

'Sir,' I said. 'As I have said already, your generosity here tonight has known no bounds, and myself and the band and the staff and all your new friends here at the Coconut Grove are extremely grateful for everything you have lavished upon us this evening ... but it behoves me as a musician to tell you that there is a limit to everything and we're NOT playing "Piano Man" again!'

A gasp went up from the bartenders. Another gasp went up from those around the Yank. And a third gasp went up from the band.

'Sorry, lads,' I say to the band. 'No way. No fucking way.'

'I know it,' Ronan says helpfully.

'Ronan, I know you know it ... and you sing it very well. But we're not doing it.'

The angry voice of our man cuts through the noise and the smoke. He mutters loudly and darkly about being insulted and then, gathering himself into a tornado of fury, he whirls his way out into the night. The bar is as quiet as if a gunfight had just taken place. Faces are frozen in horror and as they slowly reanimate, they become contorted with malevolence and anger, and it's all directed at the man who killed the golden goose. Me.

The collective anger leaves me feeling aggrieved. Am I not to be commended for honourable behaviour in the service of music? I stare out at the sea of hostile faces. In my head what I want to say is, 'What good is it for a man to pursue his destiny if along the way he must keep sacrificing his musical integrity?'

What actually comes out is, 'Ah, fuck him if he can't take a joke.'

Who says we Irish aren't a witty race?

Chapter 19

JAILHOUSE ROCK

It's Christmas. And I'm in Mountjoy Jail. What will it be like? How will the prisoners take to me? Will they be hostile from the word go? Or will I get a chance to assert myself before I become bullied or intimidated? Will they sense that I'm a timorous middle-class boy who crumbles at the first sign of physical violence?

I am escorted across the quadrangle by a warder and ushered into a corridor. With every step I take, I am drinking in as much detail as I can. The floors are highly polished and the scent of an institution is heavy in the air. The lighting is drab and the colour scheme depressing. How long, I wonder, does it take for these bland shades to rob the colour from a life?

My antennae are quivering. Is my imagination running wild or can I really hear the voices of the inmates calling out, like they do in the movies? Every footstep, every movement, seems to create an echo and the noise of a door closing in the distance reverberates through my whole body as if I am a human tuning fork.

We stop outside a door and from inside I hear a babble of voices. And then a laugh. The warder opens the door.

Inside, throwing back drinks, are prison officials and the cream of singers from the world of Irish folk, showbands and cabaret. This year the inmates of Mountjoy are going to get the best Christmas concert of their lives.

Showtime approaches. I make my way to the recreational hall. The room is still empty, but backstage behind the closed curtains a line of instruments stand poised and ready to burst into life in the hands of some of the most talented musicians in the land.

My job is to be the emcee. I will come on, tell a gag, introduce the next act and exit. Usually I include a song in my introduction, but tonight we have enough singers, so for me it will be a night of gags. I am very experienced by dint of having been the master of ceremonies at hundreds of gigs the length and breadth of the country, so I have no nerves. I am really looking forward to the novelty of playing to what is literally a captive audience.

For the inmates, it is equally a leap into the dark. The concert line-up is a lottery for them. And when you're in the pokey in downtown Dublin, you can't realistically expect to get Johnny Cash singing 'Folsom Prison Blues'. So they'll take what they can get.

The sound of footsteps and the shuffling of chairs out front let me know that our audience is assembling. I take a sneak peek through the curtains. There are inmates of every size and shape out there, a lot of them with institutional haircuts. There is a lot of good-natured joshing going on, a lot of pushing and shoving amongst themselves. There is also a frisson of tension as they constantly glance in the direction of the accompanying warders, waiting to see if the warders are clocking the monkey business that is going on.

The clock on the wall says two minutes to eight. Apart from one musician and one singer from one of the bands, there are no other artists backstage. It quickly transpires that even though this is a gig for the inmates, old showbiz habits are dying hard. Everybody is hanging back, because nobody wants to be first on stage. It's all about billing. The prisoners are not impressed and as the clock ticks on towards five past, the sound of impatient, shuffling feet seeps its way through the curtains.

When the shuffling feet turns to full foot-stomping anger, I decide to take on the mantle of martyrdom. Casting ego aside, I curse my fellow performers as I cheekily plug in an electric guitar and turn on the amp that is on stage. I'll hit them with a few good, funny songs and once the rest of them see that this is a willing audience, they'll be falling over one another to be next to perform.

I take my place centre-stage behind the curtain and, with an optimistic grin, I give the nod to the stage manager. The curtains begin to peel back. Even before they have revealed the full stage, a lone voice rings out:

'Get off, ye foo-el!'

My talent for repartee is challenged and this time it's found wanting. I blink. And in that instant, the battle is over. I struggle through three songs and lose, but even in the darkest of situations, there is gold to be mined if your lamp is working. I memorise the line and later, when RTÉ producer Joe O'Donnell dubs me 'Famous Shamus' for a children's television series called 'Hullabaloo', I use 'Get off, ye foo-el,' as a catchcry.

My second time in jail beats the hell out of my first time. Dublin's premier poet, Pat Ingoldsby, who was also one of the stars of 'Hullabaloo', is a regular visitor to St Patrick's Institution for juvenile offenders. He organises for myself and my long-time pal, Aonghus McAnally, to bring our stunning double act in to the young inmates.

We call ourselves 'Famous Shamus and Amazing Aonghus' and we have just completed The Two Eejits World Tour, a scintillating odyssey that has brought us to the Belltable Arts Centre in Limerick, the Merriman Tavern in Scariff, County Clare, and finally to the Hawk's Well theatre in Sligo town. It may not have been a big tour, but it was a happy one.

Myself and Aonghus have a lot in common. We have both presented television shows for kids. We are both from theatrical families. My father was a well-known character actor, and Aonghus's father was the famous Irish stage and international movie actor, Ray McAnally. We both have a weakness for funny songs and Aonghus is also a brilliant guitarist and a talented magician.

It is the hottest day of the year when we play the first gig of The Two Eejits World Tour at the Belltable Arts Centre. The theatre is as hot and uncomfortable as the black hole of Calcutta, but we soldier on for our forty paying customers as though we are in an air-conditioned Caesar's Palace in Las Vegas. Despite the crushing heat, we lose nobody at the interval and, gorged on our popularity, we finish the show with the two of us in bare feet, wearing nothing but a pair of shorts each.

The second gig, in Aidan O'Byrne's pub in Scariff, is a triumph. Then it's on to Sligo. We don't know it at the time, but this last gig of the tour is to be strangely prophetic. Aonghus is walking into the darkened wings of the Hawk's Well theatre when a flashlight beam lands on his feet. The beam travels up his body and stops at his face, dazzling him with its brightness.

'Are you one of them?' asks a gruff voice.

Aonghus shields his eyes from the beam and sees a policeman holding the flashlight. 'One of who?'

'Two fellas escaped from an institution in Roscommon.'

And now, here we are in St Patrick's, two fellas in an institution, about to try and entertain the juvenile offenders. They march the young men into the gymnasium and sit them down at distance of about fifteen feet from our makeshift stage. They positively bristle with hostility and it is plain to see that a lot of them are here under duress.

Fool that I am, I love a challenge, so we bravely launch into our act, and after a dour struggle for the opening twenty minutes, we are starting to get the odd smile and a laugh here and there. One wiseacre in particular seems to be a bit of a ringleader, so I focus in on him and get a bit of banter going. Before I know it, I am inviting him up on stage to sing with us.

Giving this spunky juvenile the mike is like giving him his freedom. He relishes the opportunity to abuse this unexpected platform by throwing in as many obscenities as he can, flashing a challenging glance at the warders each time he swears. Then he launches into a really raunchy version of a well-known street ballad, 'Weila Weila Walia', the story of a woman who murders her baby with a penknife 'long and sharp'. In his version the penknife has been replaced with an instrument of a completely different nature. He sings with gusto:

'She had a dildo, big and long ...'

It all goes downhill from there. From the looks on their faces, the warders are not impressed with our new lead singer, who is now ablaze with glee in his unaccustomed position of power. He finishes his song to a thunderous ovation and, never a man to look a gift horse in the mouth, I suggest an encore. And that's when The Two Eejits' scariest moment in showbiz happens.

A lad in the second row of the audience sticks his head in between the two heads in front of him and shouts in a stage whisper, 'Hey! Aonghus! Ask him about his sister the ballet dancer.'

The fella beside him in the second row leans forward and shouts, 'Don't ask him!'

The first lad tries again. 'Hey, Aonghus, go on! Ask him about his sister the ballet dancer.'

The second lad counters, 'Don't ask him.'

At this stage, I can see from his expression that Aonghus is unsure which way to play it, but he bravely goes for broke.

'What's this about your sister the ballet dancer?'

Our power-crazed, new lead singer, who has ostensibly been ignoring this whole scenario up to now, whirls violently on Aonghus. With a face like thunder he speaks in a quiet, angry voice.

'That's not funny, pal. My sister has been in a wheelchair since she was six.'

I watch the blood drain from Aonghus's six-feet-two-inch frame. Ashen and dumbstruck, he clutches his guitar to him for comfort, not knowing what to say or what to do. I'm trying to calculate the odds on us getting out alive. Will there be a prison revolt? Will The Two Eejits be taken hostage and held on the roof in the glare of the public spotlight? Will we be on the news?

Nobody moves. The silence is almost unbearable. Suddenly a grin of triumphant satisfaction breaks out on our new lead singer's face.

'It's okay, Aonghus,' he says. 'We're only messin'.'

To this day I can't figure out how they pulled it off. Nobody knew we were going to get anyone up to sing, but somehow they had put one over on us, big time. On reflection, maybe this was a routine they regularly used to wind up new prisoners. The whole audience howled with laughter. Even the warders smiled.

With the abandon of men who had faced death and lived, we tore back into them and soon we had a rollicking good show on the boil. Emboldened by this turn of events, I invited another inmate up to sing. He started into the Engelbert Humperdinck hit, 'Please Release Me', and sang a very creditable first verse. But when it came time for him to sing the words 'please release me' for a second time, he stopped and abruptly stuck the microphone back on its stand.

'Fuck this,' he said. 'All I want to do is get outta here.'

And so did we.

Chapter 20

NIGHTHAWKS

Never Put It In Writing was an awful movie made in Ireland in 1960 by the husband and wife team of Andrew and Virginia Stone. It starred the 1950s American heartthrob and crooner Pat Boone. During the shooting of the film on location at Rathmines Post Office, I was Pat Boone's stand-in for two days! I felt terribly important for a long time afterwards, even though Pat never bothered to say as much as hello.

The story involved attempts to retrieve a letter that had been posted in haste. As well as being Pat Boone's stand-in, I had one line of dialogue in a scene that involved Pat, my actor father Seamus Healy and me. It was kind of groovy to share a scene on celluloid with my Da, but I didn't get to see the movie until years later, when I serendipitously chanced upon it, buried away on a wet Sunday afternoon. It was pretty awful, but in later life the title came back to haunt me.

In the summer of 1986, I clawed my way back on television as a roving reporter on an early-evening magazine show called 'Evening Extra'. The powers-that-be were so deeply unimpressed at my return that for the entire first season I was on a week-to-week contract. The show lasted two seasons and, at the end of the second run, I co-hosted an eight-week series called 'The Dublin Village', which explored the few remaining villages within the city. It was a popular series and topped the ratings for seven of the eight-week run.

At the end of the series, I was optimistic that I would be cultivated for greater things. The exact opposite happened. I was taken aside by one of the senior programme executives and told that there was nothing for me. I was gobsmacked, insulted, hurt and angry. They had dodged telling me until the last moment and once more I was back up on the high wire without a balancing pole.

My anger got the better of me. I sat down on the spot and wrote a five-page rant to Joe Mulholland, the Controller of Programmes. I castigated the cavalier attitude the organisation displayed towards their front-of-camera personalities. I pointed out the lack of support, encouragement and compassion for us heroes of the front line. I was on a roll now and I went on to tell him that presenters were thoroughbreds who needed sensitive handling, because of our fragile nature. And so on. And so on.

When I had finished the letter, I stuck it in an envelope and, grim-faced, I hand-delivered it to the Controller's office. I then headed for the staff canteen. En route to my lunch, I bumped into a producer called David Blake-Knox. He said, 'I'd like you to front a new show I've devised, called "Nighthawks".'

That's when the title of Pat Boone's crappy movie came back to haunt me: *Never Put It In Writing*. Here I was, being offered a new series, having just deposited a hand grenade in the Controller's letterbox.

My next course of action required a clear head and expert advice, so I trundled off at speed to the office of Eoghan Harris, a fiery producer who had a divine instinct for the internal politics of the organisation. What should I do?

'Go over,' said Harris, 'and lick his arse as hard as you can.'

At six o'clock, an anxious four hours later, I found myself sitting across the desk from the Controller with my tongue at the ready.

'My letter was a little shrill ... maybe a little emotional ... hysterical ... intemperate ... foolish ... immature ...'

The Controller let me dribble to a halt.

'Well, of course,' he said, 'you are all of these things.'

Fair play to him. That was the end of the matter and the beginning of 'Nighthawks'. And the best four years of my working life.

'Nighthawks' took its inspiration from the famous Edward Hopper *Nighthawks* painting, which shows customers at a New York diner. Our 'Nighthawks' was a fictitious diner, a studio set so convincing that many viewers believed it was a real premises. The heart of the diner was a beautiful Rainbow Wurlitzer jukebox and the walls were adorned with funky pictures of film stars and musicians. It had a couple of intimate booths, a scattering of tables and stools down along the counter. A tacky plastic-strip curtain hid the tiny kitchen area from the punters' sight.

Downstairs was the 'basement', which was actually

another set right next to us in Studio 4. We had a different band playing in the 'basement' each week.

Nighthawks was a highly novel take on the standard chat show. It was broadcast live on Tuesday, Wednesday and Thursday nights. I played myself, as the owner of the diner. The talk-show guests were dotted around the diner – in booths, sitting at the counter, hanging out at a table or standing by the jukebox. The audience were invited punters who took up the remaining seats and were urged to ignore the interviews and talk and behave as though they were in a real diner.

To encourage them, they were plied with free cans of beer and the background babble of voices lent an atmosphere of informality. And because I never ever addressed the camera, a feeling was created for the audience at home that they were eavesdropping on the conversations with the guests. The cameras came to us in mid-sentence and left us mid-sentence, creating the illusion that the conversation was continuing while something else was happening on screen.

We had a couple of music numbers per show in the diner, performed by all kinds of oddballs. And, to spice up the mixture even more, some of the best funny sketches ever seen on Irish TV were interspersed between the music and the chat.

And it didn't end there. In the beginning, I had a female waitress to help me: Tanya, brilliantly played by Joanne McAteer, who dressed and spoke like the female half of an Austrian weather clock. She was my scourge, but also my muse, until her murderous Balkan boyfriend – the heavy-lidded and violent Boris, played by Stanley Townsend – came looking for her. That was the opening premise for a soap opera that was also studded throughout the show and as the show developed over four years and characters left to be replaced by other characters, the zany soap opera veered wildly from bondage in the basement to sentimentality in the kitchen.

Despite the fact that my acting might have been a little suspect, I was having the time of my life as the ringmaster. For three nights a week I revelled in the chance to display my erudition, which I always credited to a combination of a Christian Brothers' education and the *Readers Digest*. The music was left-field, the guests were left-field and the humour was as scabrous as we could make it. It was truly a collective effort and everybody in the production office chipped in ideas to take the concept to new places.

There were many special moments over the four years and the memory of them still lingers with me. One night, a well-known Irish musician, Simon Carmody, arrived out as planned, with Johnny Thunders in tow. Johnny Thunders was a member of the famous American glam-punk band, the New York Dolls. He was small and perfectly formed, wearing the obligatory black clothes and sporting a bouffant hairstyle, which had helped earn him the soubriquet of 'the Gutter Peacock'. Johnny was a paradigm of the perfect Nighthawks guest.

Unfortunately for Johnny, he had become a sad, strung-out junkie. The whiff of tragedy always makes for very compelling television, but when I went to greet him as he came into the studio in mid-show, I saw immediately that his eyes were glazed over and he didn't appear to be fully cognisant of what was going on. I made a snap judgement that we wouldn't put him on the show, but I invited him to come back the following night.

Johnny was less ragged the next night. He explained, in a distraught way, that when he had arrived from Paris the day before, he had been put through the grinder because he was in possession of methadone for his heroin habit. Any kind of hassle freaked him out and he had developed a panicky and paranoid need to know what was happening at every moment: 'What are we doing next? What are we doing after that?'

But when he came on the show, the interview with Johnny was fascinating, edgy and revealing, and when we finished talking I think he was as happy as I was that it had gone so well.

'You're going to sing a song for us, Johnny?'

'Yeah.'

'Well, you get yourself over to the microphone and get your guitar and I'll get us a bit of attention.'

Johnny headed for the performance area and I faced the punters.

'Yo, Nighthawks, I'd like you to pay attention now, as I have a little treat for you.'

Johnny looked up sharply.

'Did you call me a little creep?'

A year later, in 1991, poor old Johnny Thunders died from a methadone overdose in a New Orleans hotel room.

There were a couple of other occasions when I had to make a similar call, usually because the proposed guest had had too much drink. One night, Alex 'Hurricane' Higgins, the famous snooker player, was booked to appear. He arrived looking a bit the worse for wear. Alex was another character who gave off the same tragic vibes as Johnny Thunders. On this night he was very low, as he had just been kicked out of his home by his wife and the tabloids had had a field day. I felt sorry for him and decided he could just about handle it without making a fool of himself.

The show started and eventually I sidled over to Alex in one of the booths, where no one in the diner could hear us. The hand-held cameras gathered round us and in the style that was familiar to the viewers, the interview started in mid-sentence. It was obvious that Alex was tired and emotional, but it got worse when I asked him how important his own family in Belfast were to him. As he paid tribute to his family, bitter tears rolled down his cheeks and it was a moving few moments. About thirty seconds later, again in mid-sentence, the interview finished, the cameras drifted away and I was left facing Alex.

'Thank you, Alex,' I said. 'I realise that was tough for you.'

He looked back at me through bleary, teary eyes.

'Have we started?'

Another night one of my guests was English television

personality Lloyd Grossman, who was famous for his groundbreaking series, 'Through The Keyhole', and for several food programmes. Lloyd is a very engaging and interesting character, who has spent a lot of time in West Cork.

We decided that Lloyd and I would taste a few deep-fried crickets on air and we duly booked a chef from a popular Chinese Restaurant close to RTÉ. At the last moment, the chef cancelled and when a replacement was found, somebody gave him a less than thorough briefing. Instead of deep-frying the crickets, the new chef sautéed them in butter, so that when they were presented to us, instead of looking like crispy bacon bits, they looked like, well, sautéed insects.

Brave as two lions, Lloyd and I tackled the sautéed crickets and to say they were disgusting is to minimise what a truly ugly experience it was. Not alone did they taste foul, but a leg from one of the crickets lodged somewhere at the back of my throat and stuck there for what seemed like the next forty-eight hours.

Nighthawks' greatest moment came when the show was brilliantly manipulated by dissidents within the ruling Fianna Fáil political party and I, your humble host, was used as the blunt instrument to bring down the leader of the Government, an Taoiseach, Charles J Haughey.

In the early Eighties it was revealed that several people, including some prominent Irish journalists, had had their phones tapped with the imprimatur of the Fianna Fáil government of the day. Sean Doherty, from County Roscommon, was the Minister for Justice at that time and he took the rap, becoming in the process a combination of those two odious creatures reviled by all: the sacrificial lamb and the public scapegoat. He continued to bite the bullet for the next ten years.

In all the time we did Nighthawks, there were only two occasions on which we pre-recorded the show and the night of Sean Doherty's appearance was one of them. The fiction was that the writer and journalist John Waters believed we were to interview him in Dublin about his new book, *Dancing At The Crossroads*, so he was supposedly on his way up to Nighthawks. And I thought the interview was happening down the country in John's home area, Castlerea, in a pub called Hell's Kitchen, so we went to County Roscommon.

As Roscommon's most controversial son, it was perfectly natural for us to invite Sean Doherty on the show. It was also predictable that during the course of the interview, I was going to bring up the matter of the phone tapping. And when I said to him that he had been carrying the can for Charles Haughey for ten years, Doherty concluded his answer by saying, 'I do feel let down by the fact that people knew what I was doing'.

When the show was over and we were standing at the bar having a drink, Doherty leaned in to my ear and said, 'In case you didn't notice, I said something tonight that I've never said before.' He was marking my card in no uncertain terms.

'I hear you now,' I answered.

We returned to Dublin next morning and as soon as we reached RTÉ, I rang Bruce Arnold, one of the journalists whose phone had been tapped. I invited him to come out to the studios to have a look at the tape. As soon as he heard Doherty say the fatal words, 'I do feel let down by the fact that people knew what I was doing,' he nodded. Doherty had pulled the trigger and Nighthawks had a scoop. I glued myself to a phone and began spreading the news. I was thinking of publicity for the show, but I goofed rather badly by alerting all the newspapers but omitting to inform the RTÉ newsroom! I was not too popular.

The story exploded all over the papers next day and our show had a huge audience for the Doherty programme on Wednesday, 15 January 1992. A day later, Charles J Haughey announced his intention to resign as Taoiseach.

We thought we were great guys altogether. Our puny little entertainment fol-der-ol had brought down the most controversial Irish politician of modern times. It was only as the years passed that I came to realise that keener minds than ours had been at work. Once we had invited Sean Doherty on the show, he had anticipated correctly that I would bring up the phone tapping. After that, it was easy for him to drop the bombshell. And guess what, I was the patsy.

Sean Doherty died from a brain haemorrhage in June this year. I was surprised to read that he was only sixty; I had assumed he was several years older than me. In the aftermath of his death, PR advisor Terry Prone revealed that on the day following the Nighthawks interview, she helped Doherty prepare for his press conference, which would hammer the final nail into Haughey's coffin. She described him as being upset about what he was going to do. However, in a four-part television documentary series on Charles Haughey this year, the editor of *The Irish Times*, Geraldine Kennedy, revealed that Doherty had told her, off the record, 'I carried the can,' indicating perhaps that he had grown tired of the situation and decided to do something about it.

He stopped being the scapegoat on Nighthawks and later that night in a local hotel in Castlerea, there was nothing in his demeanour to suggest that he was upset about the coming storm. Then he said something very intriguing to me.

'Y'know something, if I'm elected next time out, it will be your fault … and if I'm NOT elected next time out, it will be your fault!'

I can never say for sure who orchestrated the whole thing. I used to think that some Machiavelli in a dissident rump of Fianna Fáil fastened on to this opportunity to bring down Charles Haughey. However, having heard Albert Reynolds say, during the course of the Haughey documentary series, that Doherty's actions were unwelcome at that time because those opposed to Haughey were confident that Haughey's number was up anyway, I am now more inclined to believe that Doherty was so aggrieved at being blamed for so long that he finally snapped and 'Nighthawks' just happened to present itself as the ideal opportunity to exact his revenge.

Either way, guess what? I was still the patsy.

Chapter 21

LACKING COMMITMENT

It's not the successful auditions that you in recall in the night, as you lie tossing and turning, trying to get to sleep. It's the failures that come to haunt you, bounding out from that dark place called embarrassment, inducing once more that clammy, eye-squinching, fist-clenching, buttock-tightening mortification that goes with not getting the gig.

In fairness, my showbiz start was highly auspicious. I cut my teeth in the Coffee Kitchen, the Old Triangle and the Universal, the three biggest folk clubs in Dublin. I fancied myself as a bit of a funnyman and I wrote humourous parodies on the events of the day.

Mick McCarthy's pub, the Embankment, was a Mecca for folkies. All the big names – the Dubliners, Paddy Reilly, Danny Doyle, Johnny McEvoy and Jim McCann – had graced the stage there. Mick himself would be emcee for the evening and would begin by telling his audience, 'My name is Mick McCarthy and I come from Lixnaw, which is a suburb of Listowel, in the county of Kerry.' Needless to remark, Lixnaw was no more than a bridge, a pub and two bicycles.

'I want to sing,' I said to Mick.

'I'll let you sing one song.'

'Will you pay me?'

'If you get an encore, I'll pay you a pound.'

Kerrymen are renowned for their cuteness, but what Mick didn't know was that my mother also came from Kerry and I was wide to an opportunity.

'Ladies and gentlemen, I'm allowed sing one song, but if I get an encore, Mick will give me a pound, so even if you don't like me, will you give me an encore anyway?'

I get my encore, I get my pound and I get myself a new friend. I am even invited to stay behind after hours and drink in Mick's kitchen. After the bar is closed, we do as much singing as we did when it was open.

In the middle of the session, Mick suddenly rises up. 'Whisht, boys and girls, everybody. The Guards are outside.' He disappears into the back room and returns within minutes, flanked by two policemen, who promptly have a couple of creamy pints of Guinness stuck securely into their hands.

My next audition comes along not long after my Embankment debut. I have become the folk writer for *Spotlight* magazine and I have also become very practised as emcee at folk gigs all over Dublin. At that time I am still working as a cameraman in RTÉ. The man who had been my boss, Mike Slevin, has moved on to being a producer and when I hear he is planning a folk show, I beseech him to give me a chance as presenter.

'Where can I see you work?'

'I'm doing a gig with the Johnstons next Wednesday in Kilkenny,' I tell him.

'Very well,' he smiles. 'I'll be out there in the dark, watching you.'

I want this gig so badly. I feel it is almost my birthright. I have to have it. All I need to do is satisfy Mike – who will be somewhere out there in the darkness.

The curtain rises and I walk out to the microphone centre-stage. I look down at the punters and there in the middle of the third row, right under the stage, as well lit as myself, is my pal Mike. He gives me a big wink. I can hardly contain myself when after the gig he says, 'The job is yours'.

Two auditions, two successes. What am I supposed to do? I promptly quit my good steady job as a cameraman, hitch myself to a runaway horse called Fame and ten years later I am still being dragged across the rocky terrain of unfulfilled ambition, when I land up for my third audition in Opryland Theme Park, Nashville, Tennessee.

A friend who works at Opryland calls me and tells me that they are looking for a ringmaster for the Animal Show. The very next day I am out there to have a look at the show. The ringmaster sings the song, 'Talk to the Animals', and he introduces the various farmyard animals, including a rooster who pulls a string that unfurls the Stars and Stripes, and a pig who blows a bugle.

Two days later I am back there, waiting to do my audition. I feel confident. Surely this will be a cakewalk? They'll be captivated by my soft Irish brogue. As I stand waiting on the stage, I feel comfortable with the microphone and I am happy that if they require me to ad lib, I have great fluency in my speech. Confidence is surging through me as I watch two guys in suits slide into the second last row of this small amphitheatre.

The backing track of the music booms out through the speakers and I begin singing. To my utter dismay I suddenly hear myself singing off-key. Whether it's nerves, or the slight echo on the microphone that is responsible, I am teetering on the brink of failure. The rooster pulls the string and the flag unfurls, but in what seems like an apt coda to this unhappy experience, the pig seems disinterested and lethargic and gives no more than a desultory toot on the bugle. For me and my prospects, it is the Last Post.

Scarified by failure, I don't audition again until fifteen years later, when word is out that they are looking for someone to play Joey 'the Lips' Fagan, the trumpet player in the movie *The Commitments*. Director Alan Parker is in town and the casting agents are two old friends, Ros and John Hubbard. I put the call in and we set a date.

This time I'm taking no chances. I read Roddy Doyle's book again and again to soak up the character. Then I try to visualise him in the persona of someone I know. I narrow it down to Johnny Murphy, a well-known character actor. Johnny Murphy is a calm character, full of surprising wisdom and generous in sharing it.

The big day comes. I have my hair cut really tight. I deliberately put on a T-shirt and a jacket that are a size too small for me and a really tight pair of drainpipe canvas jeans. They pull my torso taut. This is what I want, this tensile energy, this manifestation of coiled-spring control. I start talking like Joey as I drive my car to Ros and John's house on Lansdowne Road.

Ros greets me warmly.

'Any last-minute tips?' I ask.

'Underplay it,' she counsels. 'He likes people to under-play.'

'I'm going to play him like Johnny Murphy,' I tell her.

'That's good,' she nods.

Up in the sitting room, John has a video camera set up. There is a fine, big comfortable couch and two big arm-chairs. It is early evening and Alan Parker is sitting in shadow in the furthest corner of the room, a dark presence without a face.

'Sit down,' Ros invites me.

I sit down on the couch and instantly it swallows me. My knees are pulled up until they feel like they are half an inch from my chin. My arms are jammed by my sides and due to the position in which I am stuck, my drainpipe trousers are cutting into my balls with some ferocity.

'Tell us a bit about yourself.'

I start to babble and I hear my voice straining with nerves as I trot out my CV.

'Okay. Are you ready?'

'Yeah.'

'Okay. Let's do it.'

'Here?' I squeak. 'On the couch?'

'Yeah.'

Dear Jesus, this is not what I signed up for. Where is my lovely coiled spring? Where is my taut body ... my edgy pres-ence? What about all that great stuff where I used my hands expressively? They want me to be Joey 'the Lips' with my knees up to my chest! All scrunched up like this ... mustn't panic ... remember... underplay, underplay.

I underplay it so much that I suspect Alan Parker thinks I'm dead. Whatever energy I had coming into the room is now caught down the back of the sofa, trapped with my aching balls.

And then it's over and I'm back downstairs. I am deaf to the comforting clucking of Ros. I know how bad it has been. I get into the car, punch the wheel and shout 'Fuck' a thousand times. But at least as I drive home I draw comfort from the lesson I have learnt and I make a vow to myself that I will never, ever again do another audition.

Johnny Murphy got the part.

Chapter 22

THE MAN IN BLACK

The first time I met Johnny Cash he was on canvas. I went to live in Nashville in 1973 and, through happenstance, I found myself walking in through the front door of Johnny Cash's antebellum mansion on the lakeshore, in a place called Hendersonville, about a half-hour's drive from Nashville.

The entrance hall was wide and impressive. The bottom part of the sweeping staircase curved up from the left and the right and the two set of stairs met about fifteen feet up, on a small landing. Above the landing was a massive oil painting of Johnny and his wife, June Carter. The huge, imposing double portrait was made even more memorable by the fact that Johnny was decked out in the complete regalia of a Confederate officer and June was dolled up in a flowing ball gown. She, like her man, had a statuesque presence and a strong hint of nobility. Her pedigree came from Mother Maybelle Carter, her mother, who was considered the queen of traditional country music. Outside of seeing pictures of the carving of four American presidents' heads on Mount Rushmore, this painting remains in my memory as one of the most potent symbols of America I have ever seen.

In 1996, over twenty years on from my canvas encounter, to my great delight I am standing with a camera crew, waiting to interview Johnny Cash on the stage of a theatre in a small Missouri town called Branson.

In the wings, Johnny is in animated conversation with a man wearing a red polyester suit, black shirt, white tie, white belt and white shoes. The man's hair is swept up into a country pompadour, white but streaked with a honky-tonk, smoky, nicotine yellow. I guess that he is a singer and sure enough, on enquiry I find out his name is Ferlin Huskey.

As I watch, the two men talk and laugh and then as their conversation comes to a close, they embrace. As they draw apart, Ferlin Huskey reaches down, flips open the buckle on his white belt, slips the belt out through the loops of his trousers and hands it to Johnny Cash.

Still clutching the white belt, Johnny comes over to our crew on the stage. After introducing myself, I say to him, 'I couldn't help noticing that little tableaux with the man in the red suit.'

'That's Ferlin Huskey,' he says in his deep, sonorous drawl. 'Me and Ferlin and Elvis toured together in 1958 and me and Elvis picked up a lot from Ferlin. So we were just goin' over old times.'

'What about the white belt?' I venture.

'Well, Ferlin said to me, "I want you to have somethin' to remember me by," so he gave me his white belt.'

And then The Man in Black let go a low chuckle that rumbles from deep in his chest. 'It's the ONLY white belt I got.'

Johnny Cash, The Man In Black, turns out to be a really big
man. At six-feet-four, he towers over me, and his mane of
hair sweeps back up over his head, giving him a regal air,
in a land where there is no royalty. He has the tall and
broad physique of a warrior, a presence he enhances by
wearing long black frock coats to great effect. Like a lion,
his face is lined with scars, the result of his battles with
drink, drugs and the ravages of the road, before he finally
jumped the boundary from being an outlaw to becoming
an elder statesman.

He might not have cut it in the sophisticated North, but
below the Mason-Dixon line and all the way west, Johnny
Cash was a true American icon, a man who effortlessly
conveyed a combination of the courage of frontiersman
Davy Crockett and the gravitas of Abraham Lincoln.

Sometimes it is not a good idea to meet your heroes, in
case you find they have feet of clay. With Johnny Cash,
meeting him leaves me feeling enriched and satisfied that I
have met a true original. His warmth and humility make
interviewing him an effortless exercise and his total lack of
ego in a world full of narcissists is as refreshing as drinking
from the coolest mountain stream.

It was just and right that the last chapter in Johnny
Cash's life was a story of triumph. In the early Nineties, the
man who had given us 'I Walk The Line', 'Ring of Fire' and
'Folsom Prison' was ignominiously consigned to the

recording scrapheap by the smart, hip, new wave country radio jocks. But Johnny, bearing this slight with silent dignity, unexpectedly got a late run on the rail in the late Nineties when he fell into the lap of one of America's most influential producers, Rick Rubin, a man who was more associated with bands like the Red Hot Chili Peppers than ageing country singers.

At that stage, Johnny was so far out of vogue with the mainstream country record companies that no one saw him sneak up on them. Johnny became a truly significant independent recording artist. With Rick Rubin giving him the freedom to record anything he wanted, Johnny Cash finally reached his apotheosis with his coruscating, poignant version of the Nine Inch Nails song, 'Hurt'. He died a legend and who could begrudge him?

Lining up the interview with Johnny Cash in Branson had been no trouble to my producer, Bill Hughes. As soon as he mentioned Ireland to Johnny's manager, Lou Robin, he was pushing an open door. Johnny was very fond of Ireland. In his later years he had become great friends with the Irish singer, Sandy Kelly, and because of the friendship he played in Ireland several times in the 1990s.

But Johnny's unbreakable link to Ireland was first established when he wrote the classic 'Forty Shades of Green' in 1961. From constant repetition in interviews, the legend grew that Johnny had written his famous song after being inspired by the patchwork of green Irish fields he observed through the window of his plane as he flew over the Emerald Isle. The story sounded convincing enough and I believed it all these years until, not very long ago, my friend Tommy Higgins added a very amusing postscript. Tommy, a great country music buff, was in Canada a couple of years ago when he met the legendary Waylon Jennings.

Like Johnny Cash, Waylon had pre-eminence in country music as an outlaw, clocking up quite a few points as a hell-raiser of note. Waylon was also famous for having given up his seat to The Big Bopper on the plane that crashed and took the lives of Buddy Holly, The Big Bopper and Ritchie Valens in 1959.

Waylon grabbed his second chance at life and developed a music style that was hard-edged and tough enough to be accepted in mainstream rock clubs as well as at traditional country venues. At the start of 1961, both himself and Johnny Cash were coming out of broken marriages and when they decided to share an apartment in Nashville, this unholy domestic alliance unleashed a duo of amphetamine-fuelled desperadoes on a trail of destruction. So who is to doubt Waylon when he tells my friend Tommy that the origin of 'Forty Shades of Green' is very different from the anodyne but cute popular anecdote, as recounted by Johnny.

The way Waylon tells it, Johnny and Waylon were talking about the green Irish landscape while passing south of Ireland on a flight to London. When they got to London, they were so enthused that the two outlaws bought a map of Ireland, smoked a joint, spread the map on the hotel room floor and Johnny then wrote his way around Ireland in forty shades of 'green'.

With the two protagonists dead, there is no way to confirm the story, but the line in the song that goes, 'I'd walk from Cork to Larne to see the Forty Shades of Green,' could support the notion that the two outlaws, Mr Cash and Mr Jennings, were indeed smoking forty shades of 'green'. The walk from Cork to Larne is nothing less than a hefty two-hundred-and-fifty-mile stroll!

Before we leave Branson, let me share with you an incident that made a big impression on me.

For years, Branson, in the Ozark Mountains, was a sleepy fishing resort for middle-Americans. It had one theatre called Baldknobber's Country Cabaret, which started in 1957. Then, in 1994, a country singer with a stammer, called M-m-mel Tillis, opened his own theatre. He was followed in quick succession by a host of country music's senior citizens and in jig time, Branson became a place of pilgrimage for elderly fans of country music and a kind of elephants' graveyard for older American country singers.

When we visited it in 1996, Branson had twelve theatres that were strung out along a two-lane blacktop highway. Between every two motels there appeared to be a crazy-golf course or a kids' amusement park, but there was little evidence of kids. Branson was a kind of palsied, geriatric

American hell and for all I know, maybe the kids' enter-
tainments were aimed at those in their 'second childhood'.

But who could begrudge country greats like Charlie Pride
and Johnny Cash an audience, even if half the crowd had
dodgy prostates and the other half were taking diuretics.
There were shows in the afternoon and also in the evening. Before and after the shows, the solitary highway was
nose-to-tail gridlock. But by 10.30pm, Branson was like a
temperance town, a giant dormitory with flashing neon
lights, with everyone tucked safely into bed in the mid-
price motels.

The most famous of all the theatres in Branson belongs
to none other than Andy Williams, who lives locally for
part of the year. The Andy Williams Moon River Theatre
has an art gallery in the reception area and everything
about the place is understated and classy. As a singer, Williams is still a consummate stylist and his band is never less
than a brilliant collection of international virtuosi.

We go backstage with our camera to interview Andy in
his lavish quarters. I ask him if I can use his toilet and he
directs me down the hall. As I sit down on the toilet, I find
myself looking at an abstract painting that has a familiar
style. I look down to the bottom of the canvas and there it
is, the bold signature, *Picasso*.

I can hardly wait to dry my hands. 'Pardon me, Andy,'
sez I, 'but that painting in there, is that–?'

'Yep,' sez Andy.

A Picasso in the jacks. Now that's the classiest thing in
Branson by a mile.

Chapter 23

I WRITE THE SONGS

Songwriting was always a solitary pleasure for me until 1983, when I met Barry Mason, the man who wrote the smash hits 'Delilah' for Tom Jones and 'The Last Waltz' for Engelbert Humperdinck. We bumped into each other at the Castlebar Song Contest in County Mayo where his song pipped mine at the post to win. Barry is an affable kind of guy and when he phones me a few weeks later and proposes that we write together, I agree.

The deal is simple. I will pay for his hotel, he will pay his own airfare and the song will be a straightforward fifty/fifty split. I ring the Burlington hotel and ask them for a nice room with a view over the Dublin foothills. I pick up Barry at the airport and we chit-chat inconsequentially until we get to the hotel.

The 'nice' room is a bit of a let-down. There are two single beds and not much room between the ends of the beds and the wall. The Dublin foothills are a distant smudge on the horizon and in the cold light of day, our twin room seems more appropriate to a tawdry lovers' tryst than an attempt to create a song.

Barry has no instrument and I have my guitar. Given my

level of proficiency, whatever we are going to write will be pretty straightforward and devoid of Minor 9ths and Flattened 13ths.

'D'you write the words or the music, mate?'

'I like to do both.'

'So do I.'

Songwriters work in different ways. Some like to write a tune first and then put words to it. Others like to write a lyric and put a tune to it. Some like to write only the music. And more only write lyrics. I hear the lyrics and the music simultaneously. The rhythm of the words and the melody together dictate the tone of the song. I don't read music, so when it comes time to record a demo, I always have at least one musician who can interpret my ideas for me and be able to communicate that information to the other musicians. One thing I do know is that even though I can't write or articulate my ideas in the language of music, I hear orchestras in my head.

Barry is a kindred spirit, who also hears an orchestra in his head.

'I have an idea,' he says.

I touch a photograph, I wish it was you

I chip in:

I'm staring at your note which tells me we're through

Barry's in again:

It trembles in my hand ...

I finish the line:

... at last I understand ...

And Barry rounds it out:

The cruel and heartless things I've done to you ...

The first verse comes quickly. But if anyone had been observing the carry-on, we could have been arrested. Barry is a kind of nervy guy who likes to walk up and down while he is writing and it is having a knock-on effect on me, so that I start walking up and down as well. The cramped twin room is far from an ideal space for these peripatetic inclinations and after several collisions in the narrow space between the ends of the beds and the wall, we resort to stepping up and across the beds, like two demented Basil Fawltys, hopping from bed to bed and reversing whenever we come face to face. And this mad *pas de deux* continues until we nail the final chorus:

Tell me, tell me, tell me
That it's not too late
Tell me you'll forgive me
If I come and find you
Lost and I'm to blame
I played a losing game
I was watching the wheel going round and round
Watching the wheel going round
When I should have been watching you.

I made a good demo in Windmill Lane Studios in Dublin, but nothing happened with the song. Yet. In the songwriting business, the game is never over, because you never know at what juncture someone will 'discover' your song and decide it is perfect for their next movie.

The toughest thing in the world is to get someone to record, or 'cover' your song. The odds are stacked against you because most hit acts write their own songs, or are handed over to producers who write the songs with them and for them, so the struggle is always to try and get membership of 'the club'.

Nobody ever really knows what is going to be a hit. The failure rate in music is phenomenally high. But just as easily, it could happen that next week your first cousin might become engaged to a world famous pop star and you'll get a chance to pitch a song. The golden rule is never to pass up an opportunity. I interviewed Garth Brooks twice for a television series called 'Music City USA' and at the end of both those interviews, I handed Garth a cassette with these words:

'Garth, there is no point in me coming four thousand miles and not try to hustle you with a few songs.'

Garth hasn't recorded any of my songs. Yet. But that's not the point. I got them to him. That was a great accomplishment. I remember another time, when Glen Campbell was playing the original Grand Ole Opry in the famous Ryman Auditorium in downtown Nashville. An American movie actor friend, Jimmy Hampton, got me backstage at the gig and in my hot little hand was a cassette earmarked for Glen. I wandered down the corridor of dressing rooms backstage and came to one with Glen's name on it. The door was slightly ajar. I knocked and there was no answer. Just inside the door, I could see Glen's briefcase, standing tantalisingly open. I reached in and delicately dropped my cassette full of songs down into the briefcase and tiptoed back the way I'd come.

Just like Garth, Glen never recorded any of my songs,

but again I had at least made an effort. When I went back to Nashville in the Nineties to co-write, I got a couple of eye-openers. For starters, I saw that inside every publishing company door there is a bin. Sometimes the bin is ornate, but more often than not it is a box or a barrel with a black plastic bag in it. As each and every day goes on, the bins fill up with songs. And these are from writers who are *invited* to pitch.

In Nashville, sticking a tape into the hands of Garth Brooks is futile nowadays. He won't listen to it, and if you send it in an envelope, unless you have been invited to send it, your letter will be returned to you with a big, ugly, ink stamp on it, which says: UNSOLICITED MATERIAL. Nashville is a club and to get in you have to be invited. New writers are paired with existing members of the club and if the new writer comes up trumps, he or she joins the club and is allowed write by themselves or with the next budding genius.

Luckily, I had good contacts when I went to write in Nashville in the mid-Nineties. My friend Maura O'Connell, one of our fabulous Irish singers, who lives there, gave me a bed and lots of encouragement. My first co-write was with a thin, wiry guy about my own age, with wispy long hair. His name was Mac Gayden and he was a doctor's son. I was taking no chances on two single beds in a small room, so I hired a suite in the famous Hermitage Hotel – once the headquarters of Andrew Jackson – in downtown Nashville. Mac was unusual in that he was a Nashville native. There aren't many music business natives in Music City.

Mac already had a mega hit under his belt, called 'Everlasting Love', which is still a hugely popular song worldwide. As well as that, Mac was famous as the guitar player with the J J Cale Band and he played the famous riff on the seminal stoners song, 'Cocaine'. He had also been a member of an enormously popular and legendary musos' band called Area Code 615. With such a sweet picker in the room, there wasn't much for me to do on guitar, but it was a pleasure to find that, like Barry Mason, Mac heard the music and the lyric at the same time. We wrote two songs in about six hours and the next day we recorded demos of both songs. One was a workmanlike tune, but the other one, 'I Might Get Over You', could still come up trumps.

The skyline's in the mirror
The city's fading fast
I've got to put some distance
Between me and the past
I just crossed the county line
I only wish I knew
Just how far I'll have to go
Till I get over you

'Cos my courage is running on empty
And my broken heart is empty too
And in a hundred miles
I might get over
In a thousand miles
I might get over

In a million miles
I might get over you

My next co-write is my dream come true. My songwriting partner's name is Russell Smith and I have been a huge fan of his band, the Amazing Rhythm Aces, and in particular of one of his songs, called 'Third Rate Romance, Low Rent Rendezvous'. Russell is signed to a publishing company as a 'house writer'. Every day, someone like me is paired off with Russell to co-write. And he is just one of four writers operating to the same brief, so in that building it is possible to walk down a corridor and hear four different songs in various stages of gestation.

Russell arrives an hour late and turns out to be a small, wide-shouldered, bullfrog of a man. He has a down-homey style, but I can also sense that he will not have much patience if he thinks he is stuck with a turkey. We talk out the rules of engagement and then I throw my tuppence worth – a chorus – on the table:

When the songs start making sense
you know you're in love
And your life begins to feel like one long video
In every single word
You hear lots of new meanings that you never heard
'Cos when the songs start making sense
You know you're in love

I get the nod of approval from Russell and we write a verse. He gets a good groove going and his real skill is in making the songs sound personal. He takes a line:

Did you ever hear a song, playin' on the radio ...

and says, 'Don't say "playin' on THE radio". How about "playin' on YOUR radio"?'

Lunchtime comes and Russell has to fly to pick up his kids, so instead of lunching with my hero, I go to MacDonald's and eat my burger in Centennial Park. When we start again, we get about half of a verse written, before Russell says, 'Let's go get in the truck'. We walk out to the parking lot and climb into Russell's pick-up truck. As we drive away, he pulls out a fine, big, fat joint, which we proceed to demolish.

The smoke makes Russell more talkative and he apologises about having to run off at lunchtime. His wife has just left him for another woman and he has fought to hold on to his kids. He has no forgiveness in his heart, but he feels he has started to recover because he is developing a sense of humour about it, and says he was highly amused at the last meeting with the lawyers to see his wife, rather than him, eyeing up the pretty secretary.

We return to our labours, but I am off my head and I am too busy concentrating on holding myself together to be of much use to anyone. We agree to continue a few days later. I am so stoned that I need to focus on something to mellow me out. I go to the movies to see Daniel Day Lewis in *The Last of The Mohicans*. It is a bad choice. As Daniel and his Mohican friends run through the woods, every snap of every twig seems to reverberate at colossal volume in my head.

When we do get together again, Russell has a great idea for the song, but before we get much done, once again,

Russell says the dreaded words, Llet's get in the truck'. Once more, out comes a spliff and once more I am wasted on his very strong grass. We record a very crude demo of the song and then he is gone and yet again I am terribly stoned and in need of focus. This time I go to see Gerard Depardieu in *Columbus*. I wake up just as 'The End' flashes up on the screen.

Never say die. My third co-writing partner is a big, fat good ole boy called Joe Chambers. He owns a guitar store in Murfreesboro, a small town about thirty miles from Nashville. I can't miss the store, as it has a thirty-foot-high Fender electric guitar standing upright outside the shop. Joe has a couple of country number 1 hits under his belt and he played the piano on 'Stand By Your Man', Tammy Wynette's big hit, as well as being the piano player of Charlie Rich's two big 1970s hits, 'Behind Closed Doors' and 'The Most Beautiful Girl In The World'.

Joe's store has a welcoming feel to it. There are a couple of big, comfortable couches in the midst of the clutter of guitars and amps. He sits me down on a couch, sticks a guitar in my hand and grabs one for himself. As usual, I have a chorus and this time it is an unusual chorus to an unusual song, 'Superman, Moses and Me'.

My friend in Nashville, Pat Wilson, has an adopted son, Jimmy. When he was about six, he came to her and said, 'Mom, I don't mind being adopted'.

'Why not?'

'Because there's Superman, Moses and me.'

The idea of the three adopted kids had stuck in my head for a long time, so myself and Joe began kicking it around and decided the song would be about a father trying to break the news to his son that he is adopted:

I stumbled through words I'd rehearsed in my head
So many times before
He turned to me and he said with a smile
'Dad, you don't have to say any more
Y'see I've known the story for such a long time
From a letter I found on a shelf
And I'm not going lookin' for where I came from
'Cos you loved me more than anyone else.

While we are writing this first verse and chorus, Joe takes time out to sell a guitar and a Wah Wah pedal. He is fascinating to watch as he sidewinds his way towards his customers, as if any sudden move might spook them. If there is such a thing as a low-pressure sales pitch, Joe has it in spades.

Joe orders lunch – two sandwiches for him, one for me. As we talk about this and that, he takes orders on the phone and sells another guitar. And then we take advantage of a lull to finish our song:

I didn't fall from the Heavens
Like a star falling out of the night
And I wasn't hid in a basket
In the rushes to keep me from sight
But you've always made me feel special
Like a gift from the good Lord above
And I'm not goin
'Cos you never held back on your love

And I've always been happy to be who I am
I'm in good com-pany
'Cos not many people come into this world
Like Superman, Moses and Me.

My laid-back time with Joe Chambers is in stark contrast to my time with Barry Mason all those years ago. I am very happy with our collaboration, which feels like it has happened organically. We exchange a big, warm handshake and I hit the road for Nashville.

Next day I roll up to Clark Williams's one-man demo studio, the Delivery Room. Clark is about my own age. His voice is somewhere between Elvis and Marty Robbins and sounds very pleasing to my ear. Clark plays all the instruments and in a couple of hours we have recorded the song and we are ready to mix. As we fine-tune our mix, Clark's heartbreaking story emerges.

'I was signed to three different record labels, Warner Brothers, Capitol and Atlantic, and each time the person who signed me was either fired or moved on. I never got to release a record.'

Clark is resigned to singing demos for the rest of his days and from a selfish point of view, he does a fine job on 'Superman, Moses and Me'. So far, nobody has recorded the song, but I never leave home without it. Just in case.

But as my touchstone for pitching songs, I always go back to the pastor who married one of my producer buddies, Steve Buckingham, who has been Dolly Parton's producer for the past twenty years.

'We were up on the altar, in the middle of the ceremony,' recalls Steve, 'and the next thing I feel the pastor slip something into my pocket. When I get a chance to examine it later, it's a cassette of his songs!'

Good man, the pastor.

Chapter 24

BEING JIM BRADY

By way of complete contrast to the long-fingering Justin and his slow-to-part-with-money ilk on the Irish circuit, let me tell you about the time I got paid before I had even sung a note. In fact, Shay Healy never even performed that night – stay with me on this, all will be revealed in good time.

The Nashville skyline slides slowly out of my rear view mirror and with it goes the memory of yet another adventure. I am leaving Music City after two years, with nothing to show for my efforts but the Buick Le Sabre under me. In my songwriter's romantic imagination, the car has become my pony, as I gallop off across the prairie in search of another town.

The truth is I am rolling north up Highway 65, heading for Boston, 1500 miles away, on a half-promise of some work from my friend Bill Carson. I don't deserve him as a friend. The man who had brought me to Nashville had caused Bill great hurt and I had sided with the asshole. It was a clumsy act of disloyalty on my part, but Bill is bigger than my offence and has forgiven me.

My route is taking me up through Louisville, home of

Muhammad Ali, or Cassius Clay as he was known in his younger days in Louisville. Along with so many others, all my life I have been in thrall to the legend of Muhammad Ali. But I never knew how much, until one day at LAX airport in Los Angeles, Muhammad Ali walked into my eyeline at a distance of about fifty yards. An incredible impulse gripped me. The pull of the gravity of this great star was sucking me in. I felt myself begin to run towards him, first slowly and then quickening as I got closer. And then I was shaking hands with him and he was smiling at me and giving me his autograph.

After our encounter, my hands were trembling and the adrenaline was whizzing around my body at a million miles an hour. I felt totally elated and satisfied in a way I have never fully understood, at the time or since, because up to that point in my life I had met several movie stars and a lot of stars from the music world, but I had never before felt the compulsion to run to them and touch their hems.

Louisville and memories of Muhammad Ali fade behind me. I put the boot down and don't stop again until I reach Cleveland, a drab city sitting on the mighty Ohio River. In my pocket I have a piece of paper with the name of a club where I might get a gig. The owner is warm and welcoming and offers me a gig, but not until the following night. What the heck. I put in the night, slowly sipping on a beer and then I sleep in the car, 'down by the banks of the Ohio'. Next day, when I tell people what I have done, they look at me like I am nuts and inform me I am lucky I haven't been murdered in my sleep.

With the gods apparently on my side and secure in the knowledge that I will be paid for the gig, I book into the YMCA and good fortune rewards me with a room high up in the building with a panoramic view over the city. I spend the day exploring Cleveland, becoming ever more curious at the sight of so many young rockers converging on the city. The mystery is solved when I get close enough to read their T-shirts. The Rolling Stones are making their debut in Cleveland this very evening. And so am I!

I'm not sure whether to feel chuffed or dismayed. Here I am, going head-to-head with Mick Jagger! I decide on feeling chuffed and I retire to my eyrie to watch the anticipated crowd of 85,000 Rolling Stones fans gather in the streets below.

The songwriter in me can't resist it. Out comes my 'sure hit' songwriter's pen:

I made my debut in Cleveland,
Up against the Rolling Stones
They had a famous reputation
I was strictly an unknown
But I can be exactly like Mick Jagger
I can pout and be a bitch like him
It's trying to convince the fickle public
And that's like trying to teach a dolphin how to swim

And here I am in Cleveland
Up against the Rolling Stones ...

My gig in the club is a thing of joy. I am on top form and

I wonder for an instant how Mick and the boys are doing in the stadium across town. I share my thoughts with my audience of two hundred and four and with a bit of nudging from me, we unanimously conclude that they wouldn't have had half the craic had they gone to the Rolling Stones.

Back in the YMCA I write the final chorus:

So here I am in Cleveland
Up against the Rolling Stones
They've eighty-five thousand or more
Last count we had us just two hundred and four
I look into the streets of the city
And all the pretty ladies I see
But they've all come to see the Rolling Stones
And nobody has come to see me.

By the time I hit Springfield, Massachusetts, next day, I am getting into a Boston frame of mind. I've been reading Peter Benchley's book, *Jaws*, along the way and soon I will see the sea for the first time in two years. I grew up so close to the sea in Dublin that the rhythm of the tide has always been in my blood. And even though Nashville had plenty of lakes and the Cumberland River as well, I was always conscious of being landlocked. Now I've reached Boston and I am driving along Woolaston Beach and the waves rolling in are a joy to my heart. But they are also a sad reminder that Ireland is so far away and I'm broke and jobless.

Bill Carson greets me warily. Again I offer him my

sincere apologies for siding with the asshole in Nashville and pretty soon he is smiling enthusiastically and doing what he does best – organising other peoples' lives.

'Did you ever meet Jim Brady?' he asks.

'I don't think so.'

'D'you wanna be Jim Brady tomorrow night?'

Jim Brady, he tells me, is a Boston Irish entertainer who has been booked at a fee of four hundred dollars to play at five o'clock the following evening, in a pub in downtown Boston, at a fund-raiser reception for James Michael Connolly, a Boston city councillor. Except Jim Brady can't do it.

'Nobody there knows what Jim Brady looks like,' says Bill. 'It's the easiest money you'll ever make. And if you fuck up, they'll blame Jim Brady! You can't lose. Two musicians will meet you at the gig, a bass player and a drummer. You give them a hundred dollars each and pocket two hundred for yourself.'

There is no arguing with that kind of money. Besides which, I am not making much headway as myself, so it mightn't be any harm to see how I fare as somebody else. As I pack my trusty Ovation guitar into the trunk of the Buick, the circular nature of life gives me a little jolt, reminding me that I had bought this very same guitar from Bill in 1972.

As soon as I get to the pub in downtown Boston, I locate the manager.

'I'm Jim Brady,' I announce. When he doesn't contradict me, I brazenly attempt a Boston accent, which I have been practising in the car on the journey by saying over and over, 'The kah is paahked in Haarvad Yahrd.'

My faux Boston accent is convincing enough for the manager to pull a cheque out of his shirt pocket and hand it to me along with a ballpoint pen.

'I won't be here when you finish, so if you want to sign this cheque, I'll cash it for you now.'

He hands me a cheque for four hundred dollars made out to Jim Brady. I sign it with an illegible squiggle and wonder to myself if all Jim Brady's gigs go this smoothly. For a brief moment I toy with the idea of changing my gigging name to Jim Brady on a permanent basis. The manager hands me four crisp hundred-dollar notes. I thank him profusely. Then I check the mikes and the sound system. Everything is hunky dory and it is about time for me to go outside and wait for the two musicians. There is no way they can miss me in my yellow trousers, my white shirt and my green cap.

A green Cheverolet station wagon comes gliding up to the kerb. The front doors open and out step two twenty-year-olds in immaculate tuxedos. Their frilly shirtfronts have Kelly green frosting along the edges. It is going to be an incongruous sartorial mix between my canvas yellow jeans, my white linen shirt, my green tweed cap and two college boys in tuxedos, but with the two of them dressed identically, it has a curious kind of symmetry. We look at each other and a grin breaks the ice as we shake hands.

'I'm Jim Brady,' trips off my tongue. I'm getting very comfortable with this lie.

'I'm Rick.'

'And I'm Danny.'

Rick, with the un-Irish name, is the one with the Irish background. Danny is from an Italian family. A bit of gentle interrogation yields up the extent of their joint previous experience with Irish music. Rick has done one Irish gig. Danny is a virgin. It is no time to panic.

'Okay, guys. Here's what we do. I'll start each tune on my own, to give you the rhythm and the key and then you guys join in whenever you think you have it.'

With our battle plan drawn up, I give them the good news that they are being paid in advance. They are as incredulous as I had been and, from a psychological point of view, I have now harnessed the turbine of their desire to do the best they can for Jim Brady. They set up the drums and bass on stage and I wait for the manager's signal.

The pub is quickly filling with men in business suits. And women in business suits. There is a lot of raucous glad-handing and backslapping going on and it is with great relief that I suddenly realise that Jim Brady is here simply as background noise. What a silly old Jim Brady I am not to have twigged this sooner!

At precisely five o'clock, the manager gives me the nod. I begin to strum 'The Irish Rover' and, tipping a wink to the Rick and Danny, I turn back into the mike.

'Good evening ladies and gentlemen. My name is Jim Brady and this is my band, Tuxedo Junction.'

Chapter 25

SLIPPED DISCS

In 1979, Billy Connolly sang one of my songs, 'The Country & Western Supersong', on Michael Parkinson's chat show on the BBC and during his interview he gave me a name check as the writer. Well, it was like being blessed by the Pope, even though, on reflection, it would be hard to find two people further apart than the Big Yin and His Holiness.

'The Country & Western Supersong' is a piss-take of country music, and in this exaggerated saga everybody comes to a sticky end. Here's the first verse:

Oh me Granny is a cripple in Ireland
And the story I'll tell you is true
One day she went out in her wheelchair
Didn't know that it had a loose screw
Then the wheel it fell off of her wheelchair
And on three wheels it trundled away
And it kept on rolling on over a cliff
In a seaside resort far away

Yodel-ay-ee

Yodel-ay-ee
Yodel-ay-ee ...

When I first recorded the song in 1972, it was deemed unplayable by Radio Éireann. They felt that their listeners' ears were too delicate for such irreverent lampoonery. Five years later, the well-known Irish comic and actor, Des Keogh, recorded his version. He was quietly banned as well. But, surprise, surprise, when Billy Connolly made it fashionable, the taboo was lifted, proving again the old saying that it is hard for a man to turn a profit in his own land.

Although I made very little profit out of my own recording, I had a lot of fun. 'The Country & Western Supersong' was the lead track on a four-track Extended Play record, or an EP as it was called back then. The other tracks were 'The Duodenal Waltz', an *homage* to an ulcer; 'The Mooing Behind The Hill', the sad story of a lovesick cow, and it finished with 'The Kilmuckridge Hunt', a stirring waltz-time account of the local hunt club in the seaside Wexford town:

So if ever you go to Kilmuckridge
Do you think you could show them know-how
For the Kilmuckridge Hunt
They all ride back-to-front
On three donkeys, two dogs and a cow ...

It was the musicality of the name Kilmuckridge that sucked me in, but I had never physically been there when

I wrote the song. The song mentions Ned Cotter and Mooney, two entirely fictitious characters, but when I did finally make it to Kilmuckridge for the first time, I was taken aside by a posh lady, who said to me in conspiratorial tones, 'We all love your song. And we recognise everybody in it!'

Five years passed before I made another record. The long gap was an act of mercy on my part. I knew I had more of a style than a voice. My Da used to say, 'Son, you sing like Carl Rosa ... and he's been dead for thirty years.'

Then in 1977, a great journalist and wag, Paddy Murray, wrote a delicious parody of the country song 'Lucille', which proved irresistible to me:

> *You picked a fine time to knee me Lucille*
> *Right in the nuts*
> *You don't know how it feels ...*

It may have been irresistible to me, but it was eminently resistible to the public. However, success was just around the corner. I teamed up with musician and record executive, Dave Pennefather, to become a two-man band called Rubbish. We recorded a parody of ABBA's hit song, 'Mama Mia', in the vernacular of two Dublin gossips:

> *Hey C'mia*
> *Did ye hear about our friend in*
> *No. 47*
> *Hey C'mia*
> *I hear she's havin' an affair with*

The man from the insurance
Yeah
I hear they're at it every night
I wonder what he tells his wife
My
My
He ought to be ashamed now ...

It had taken a lot of persuasion before we had wrung permission to record it from ABBA's publishers. Some time later, a sound-alike orchestral tape of ABBA backing tracks was given to me by an impresario friend, Oliver Barry. I wrote ten more parodies of ABBA songs to fit the backing tracks and I got Chips, the finest pop band in the land, to record them, dead straight. We had 'Sox', about smelly socks, 'Ring Ring', which was about Quasimodo, 'Snow On Me, Snow On You', and my personal favourite, the ultimate toilet humour, 'What-A-Loo':

What-a-loo
Classical paintings on the wall
What-a-loo
Mother of pearl handles on the door
What-a-loo
Floor done in tiles of green and blue
What-a-loo
What a nice place it is
What-a-loo
Oh woh woh woh
What-a-loo

What a nice place it is
What-a-loo

This time the publishers wouldn't budge. 'ABBA didn't like them' was the official verdict. I was so disappointed because I had intended to parody the cover of the famous ABBA album which had a picture of the two couples on a park bench. I planned to hang my singers from meat hooks and call the album ABBAtoir.

But I was never a quitter, so I waited until ABBA came to play in Dublin. At the after-gig party I was introduced to Benny. He would understand.

'Benny,' sez I, 'Did you ever hear the album of ABBA parodies?'

'No.'

'Well, can I send it to you?'

'Sure.'

So I sent a tape to Benny. And guess what? I'm still waiting to hear from him. Twenty years later.

Rubbish had their one and only hit with 'Hey C'mia', reaching No. 2 in the Irish Top 10. It was merely coincidence that at that time I was writing for the magazine that compiled the charts. Our most memorable gig as Rubbish was in the library of the snooty Royal Dublin Society, famed as the venue for the annual international showjumping competition, the Aga Khan Trophy.

The RDS library is literally a book-lined auditorium. There are two lighting changes available: On and Off. We are the most inappropriate opening act ever for the star attraction, Scottish tenor Kenneth McKellar. Dave

Pennefather is wearing a gingham dress, with a matching bonnet. I chose to be a sailor and for extra madness we have drafted in, on keyboards, Alan Dee dressed as a Light Hussar. It becomes clear to us very quickly that the audience and Rubbish come from separate planets. But that has never fazed us before, so why should we let it worry us now?

About halfway through the third song of our slightly rude programme, I perceive a middle-age woman in a tweed suit clumping up the centre aisle in her sensible shoes. She has steel-grey hair over two flinty eyes and a grim line of a mouth. She determinedly deposits a note at my feet.

'WE'VE HAD ENOUGH OF YOUR FILTH. PLEASE GET OFF.'

Now we have a hostile audience and still a stretch to go. I modify our set list and we steer a safe passage until our last song, 'The Unicorn'. The final line of the song goes: 'And that's why you'll never see a unicorn to this very day.'

Caution is now thrown to the wind.

'But that's okay with the folks here at the RDS,' sez I. 'After all, who needs a horny horse hanging around in the middle of your famous Horse Show?'

Shortly afterwards, Rubbish received a formal letter from the RDS to tell us that we were banned for life. By our reckoning we got off lightly, so we promptly changed our name to Crack and had a tilt at the British charts with a song about Paul McCartney's unfortunate detention in a Japanese jail for attempting to import a half pound of grass. It was called 'Silly Fellow'. The record reached No.

100 in the British Top 100 and there it stayed.

Here I am in Tokyo
With nothing left to smoke, I know
That I have been a really silly man
Soon as we had touched the ground
They quickly found me half a pound
They said 'we don't allow this in Japan'
I said, it's for myself you know
They looked at me and said 'Ah, so!'
I felt like one as they led me away
They put me in a prison cell
Took my guitar away as well
I wish that I had wings to fly away

I am such a silly fellow
Always trying to be mellow
When I should be upright and be free
I am such a silly fellow
Now these people
Small and handsome
They are really getting mad at me

After 'What's Another Year' won the Eurovision Song
Contest in 1980 everything changed. As the money rolled
in, I became a dilettante recording artist and I recorded
what I thought was a clever, ironic and amusing hymn to
Armageddon, 'It's Almost 1984'. I performed it on 'The Late
Late Show', but no one cared. However, fired with the passion of an arriviste, I didn't care either. I was spending

money like a drunken sailor. Then my sadly lamented friend, the late Dermot Morgan, said, 'Here's a line for a song'. How could I resist? The line went:

If I were Sebastian Coe I think I'd run a mile from you ...

Sebastian Coe was England's most brilliant middle-distance runner ever. In August 1981 he set a new World Record for the mile, running it in an astonishing 3.47.33 seconds. The song wrote itself in about fifteen minutes:

If I were Sebastian Coe I think I'd run a mile from you
Every step I take would be a pleasure from my point
of view
In 3 mins 47.33 seconds there would be an end to my
blues
'Cos if I were Sebastian Coe, Coe, Coe
If I were Sebastian Coe, Coe, Coe
If I were Sebastian Coe, Coe, Coe
I think I'd run a mile from you.

The song lasted exactly 3.47.33 seconds. This was my gimmick. My sales pitch said:

'Put this record on your turntable, open your door, run a mile ... and if you get back to your house before the record is finished, you have just broken the World Record.'

I generously sent a copy to Sebastian's 'people' and they told my 'people' that if I released it in England and tried to associate Sebastian with it in any way, they would promptly have me in court. Gratitude how are ye!

My next stab at being a recording star was another case of piggy-backing. The well-known Irish country singer, Susan McCann, had a hit with a song called 'Bob Wills is Still the King', a paean of praise to the King of Texas Swing. I cast around in my brain to see who in Irish show-business might merit an equal song of praise and after a short deliberation, I settled on Big Tom McBride, a giant of a man with a craggy face and a head that appeared to be one size too small for the rest of his body.

Big Tom and the Mainliners were a Country 'n' Irish band who hailed from Castleblayney, County Monaghan. There is a great apocryphal story doing the rounds that tells of how Big Tom and the Mainliners were advertised to play in Chicago and because of the connotations of their name, the crowd of eager punters who turned up to see the band were junkies to a man.

Big Tom lived the life of a country star and even had guitars incorporated into his wrought-iron gates. His biggest hit was a song called 'Gentle Mother', a maudlin dirge which catapulted him into the front ranks of Ireland's most popular entertainers and had him filling ballrooms and marquees to bursting point.

A marquee in the middle of a field was a prominent feature of Irish dancing life in the summer months in rural areas. Many bands were measured in the past on their ability to fill either a 'two-poler' or a 'three-poler'. Big Tom had no trouble filling a 'three-poler' and people still speak in awe of one particular marquee that was so crowded, that not alone did they have to close the entrance to the tent, they also had to close the gate to the field!

I changed the angle of praise slightly and wrote a song called 'Big Tom will Make Me a Star'. And I gave Susan McCann a mention as well:

Big Tom will make me
Big Tom will make me
Big Tom will make me a star
Ask Susan McCann
He's your only man
If you're ever going to go far ...

Big Tom failed to make me a star, so I went into a huff for a couple of years until 1985, when I tried yet another record. It was a cover of a Tom Paxton song called 'Wasn't That a Party', which was released for me by my old friend Noel Carty. Nobody showed up for the party.

About that same time, I was singing a parody of Lou Reed's 'Walk on the Wild Side' and it was proving to be a winner as a live performance. My version was called 'Walk on the Northside', and it told the story of a Southside namby-pamby who falls for a girl from the grittier Northside of Dublin, only to have his Daddy's car stolen by joyriders.

... and the joyriders go
Beep de beep
Beep beep de beep
At the Gardaí ...

There had been a few tragic fatalities in an epidemic of

joyriding and although it wasn't my intention to make light of these tragedies, as a humourist, I had granted myself an artistic license to make fun of whatever I felt like. However, a female relation of a victim heard I was due to perform in a hotel on the Northside and wrote me a strong letter of complaint, which insinuated that some form of protest might take place at the gig.

The Northside hotel was my first essay into hostile territory for fifteen years so I felt mild trepidation at the prospect of a protest. However, I launched into them and had a good head of steam built up when I went into my introduction to 'Walk on the Northside'.

Almost immediately, an angry, middle-aged woman rose to her feet and stomped towards the stage. Shades of the RDS all over again. I stopped in my tracks and watched helplessly as she climbed onto the very low stage. She was surely the mother of some hapless joyriding victim and I was about to be castigated for my insensitivity. Arms flailing, she began to address the audience:

'I don't think it is right that Shay Healy should be allowed to come over from the Southside and start slaggin' the good people on the Northside.'

She paused for effect. And then, to the utter astonishment and delight of me and the band, the punters in unison shouted, 'Ah, fuck off'.

I recorded 'Walk on the Northside', and even though it was probably my biggest potential hit, because I am sometimes wilfully perverse, I never released it. It was almost like if it was going to be a hit, then it would ruin a consistent run of flops.

At that point I took a vow to walk away from recording, but in 1986, when there was very little going right for me, I suffered an anxiety attack and unbidden, I found myself carrying the cross of Ireland's campaign to shut down the Sellafield nuclear plant in Cumbria in North Wales. I wrote a song called 'Fish that Glow in the Dark' and announced my grandiose plan to collect a million signatures, despite the fact that all the evidence so far had confirmed that I couldn't sell a couple of hundred records.

When Noah sailed out on the deluge
He never imagined the fish swimming under the Ark
Would one day glow in the dark ...

This time the gimmick was a sleeve that incorporated a luminous fish. I was genuinely wound up to an intense degree and zealously blagged my way on to radio stations down the west coast of Britain and Wales, where I denounced all nuclear scientists as arrogant pigs. I ended up with about eighty thousand signatures, a bad case of the blues and a firm resolve to stay away from recording studios.

When my grandson Fionn was born in 1993, making another record never crossed my mind until I started singing to him and with him. I had such an enjoyable time that, a couple of years ago, I recorded a CD of animal songs for kids called 'Havananimalweek'. If I couldn't get the money from the parents, I reasoned, I would take the money from their kids instead.

The CD took a ferocious spurt in its first two weeks and

the trade was predicting that I would have a Christmas hit. But the kids must have inherited their taste from their parents and they stopped buying. Sales quickly ground to an ingnominious halt.

So that's it. I've quit making records.

For the moment.

Chapter 26

MY CHINA GIRL

Tiananmen Square is a vast space, bigger and wider in its actuality than cameras can ever convey. I close my eyes and try to imagine it full of people. It is three weeks since the first anniversary of the notorious massacre of 4 June 1990, when the army opened fire on a crowd of unarmed protesters. The unobtrusive, white security cameras dotted around the square are a subtle reminder that China is a totalitarian state.

Apart from a few native Chinese stragglers, the only people on the square right now are Declan Farrell, director and cameraman, Liam Lavelle, sound and technical supervisor, me, big mouth and show-off, and our female Chinese interpreter, Pei Siu.

Pei Siu glances furtively around before she whispers out of the side of her mouth, 'I knew the soldiers were going to fire.' She is the only native so far to offer any opinion. Everyone else is too terrified to talk. The police have eyes and ears everywhere. An Irishman, Sean Riordan, had told us earlier that on the night of the massacre he had seen lots of bodies and could hear bullets whizzing through the night, thudding against the outside of his apartment block, breaking windows and leaving deep gouges in the concrete.

Our mission to China is adventurous to say the least. One of my old friends from the music business, Richard Gillinson, has popped up yet again in my life, this time with a Chinese pop singer called Wei Wei in tow. The plan is to film the first half of a documentary about Wei Wei, showing her in concert, at home, in the recording studio and on the streets of Beijing. The second half of the documentary will be shot in England when Wei Wei gets a deal from a British record company.

We have been refused permission to bring our video camera to Tiananmen Square, but it is a moot point as the authorities have impounded all our equipment and have been holding it at the airport for the past three days. According to them, we do not have the 'right papers'. The man who has got us into China and should have ensured that we had the right papers, is an English freebooter called Tim Dyson, who has been recommended to Richard as a good 'fixer'.

Dyson is a big man, with the florid complexion of someone who is fond of drink. He uses his bulk as he towers over the natives, treating them with a complete lack of respect, shouting at them in his quasi-posh voice. Shyster that he is, he blames the bungling authorities for giving us the 'wrong' papers, so in the face of Dyson's lack of clout, we have mobilised an army of people with influence, led by Eamonn Robinson from the Irish Embassy. People with influence command great respect in China. People without influence are dirt.

There is one other major precondition to our trip. In order to finance our travel expenses, I have got us an advance of £10,000 from RTÉ television. In return for the money, we have promised to deliver a half-hour feature to be entitled 'Shay Healy's Beijing'.

Since the Tiananmen Square massacre, China is not exactly on the list of favoured destinations, so the Air China jumbo is empty on the flight over. There are more cabin staff than passengers and we have the luxury of rows and rows of seats on which to stretch out. When we arrive, Beijing Airport is also decidedly unbusy and everything goes smoothly until they inform us that our camera and sound equipment is being impounded. Reluctantly, we take a taxi to our hotel and immediately set about trying to spring the gear.

From the taxi, the first impression of Beijing is of a low-rise, vast city, with huge, wide boulevards and not much traffic. The closer we get to the centre of the city, the more the preponderance of bicycles begins to dominate. We see every conceivable kind of two- and three-wheelers, as bikes whizz to and fro in the traffic. Some bikes carry solitary cyclists, more are pulling small carts with children or animals on board. Even more extraordinary are the tricycles, some pulling small flatbed four-wheelers stacked high with furniture. And it all moves in concert, with no crashes and no road rage.

We are staying at the Jianguo hotel, a stylish, modern establishment, which is much favoured by ex-pats and embassy staff. We check in, dump our bags and go downstairs to meet our popstar, Wei Wei.

Wei Wei is a slim, pretty, twenty-one year old, with her hair cut in a boyish crop. She wears casual western clothes. Her eyes are feline and sexy and she speaks a small amount of strained English in a sultry growl. With her is Madam Jiang from the Ministry of Culture, Mr Ma and Mr Liu. Madam Jiang is in charge of keeping an eye on Wei Wei for the duration of our visit. Straight away, Madam Jiang lets us know that China is the oldest civilisation in the world, with five thousand unbroken years of culture. She explains that Wei Wei belongs to a working collective and that she must contribute a percentage of her income for the greater good of her workmates. She is also obliged to perform at a certain number of concerts for the workers and she tells us that in a few days' time we will be allowed to film Wei Wei performing at a concert for the Construction Workers.

Mr Ma, Head of Propaganda Planning, is small, squat and tough-looking, and whenever we are filming he is to be our constant companion. We decide he is a member of the Secret Police, taciturn and inscrutable to the point of parody. Mr Liu makes up the trio of government officials.

Our interpreter, Pei Siu, studied at Oxford and her English is good. She translates for us, but all the time I am wondering if she understands the concept of *craic*, as we know it. And more importantly, can she in turn convey this information to the grim-faced trio. Can she explain that we are not interested in the politics of China and only interested in music and levity?

I never feel less than emasculated when I am unable to speak the language of a foreign country. Stripped of my bullshit and verbal dexterity, I become a helpless eunuch, rolling my eyes, waving my arms about ineffectually, as I try to communicate. On the plus side, Declan, Liam and I all speak fluent Irish, which we are confident none of our hosts will be able to comprehend. It is our secret weapon and it will prove very useful as the story unfolds.

Madam Jiang and her cohorts leave us and we are joined by Jim Dornan and his partner, Breda Ryan from Wexford. Jim is the boss-man of Coca Cola in China and because of that he has great connections. We are also joined by a Scotsman, Ron Kidd, editor of a newspaper called *China Daily*. He is one of six westerners who live in the massive *People's Daily* newspaper compound in the city, along with 3,000 Chinese workers. Ron is hoping to marry a Chinese woman, Xia Jiu, but the authorities are very disapproving of such relationships and her punishment, if she goes ahead and marries Ron, is that she will lose her job. Ron is angry and bitter.

'Don't ever forget that China is a totalitarian state,' he hisses. 'Never set them up.'

This is an expensive bit of information, as in the next breath Ron borrows $300 from us. We will see a lot more of Ron over the coming days.

Our first full day has slipped by and still we have no equipment. Jim Dornan arranges a meeting with Li An Min, a bigwig in a government company called Citic, which oversees joint-venture projects with western companies. The boom in China is slowly starting to happen. Li An Min exudes power and he promises to become our ally in getting our gear for us. After a delicious lunch, we go to see the Citic shop. I buy two silk dressing gowns at a cost of about £5. When I am not offered any discount, our English buccaneer, Tim Dyson, goes mad and begins shouting abusively at the manager. We are ushered into a gloomy, Dickensian office and over endless glasses of Sprite, we talk about our honour, their honour and how no insult was intended by either side. I get my discount and as a bonus, we all get a free T-shirt.

Free T-shirts are no substitute for our equipment. Our chances of having enough time to shoot the documentary and 'Shay Healy's Beijing' are dwindling with each passing hour. Declan, Liam and myself decide on a bold plan. Instead of my personal view of Beijing, we will do a 'Nighthawks in Beijing'. The Nighthawks format is very informal and mixes interviews, music, comedy and a little bit of soap opera in a restaurant setting, against a background of real restaurant chatter. If we can organise it, it means that, logistically, we can pull a lot of people together in one place and play catch-up on our filming.

Pei Siu's uncle cooks a stunning night-time feast for us, which includes deep-fried scorpions on a bed of crispy white noodles. Apart from a tiny soft spot on the breastplate, the little critters are extremely crunchy and tasty. Having dined adventurously, we run the idea of 'Nighthawks in Beijing' past Pei Siu. She brings us to the Ren Ren restaurant, where we listen to some local cabaret singers caterwauling doleful dirges. We talk to the manager, Mr Wong, and provisionally book the restaurant for Friday night. We also ask him if he can cook us a snake.

The next day I return with Pei Siu and we have quite a

gathering in Mr Wong's office. The day manager and his assistant are there; so too are the night manager and his assistant. The general manager and his assistant have also shown up. And on the table, in a wire basket, are two three-foot snakes.

Even though I am unable to speak the language, my prescience is about to come in very handy. In a moment of inspiration before I left home, I had photocopied a very small map of the world, which showed China about the size of the tip of your little finger and Ireland, by comparison, the size of a full stop. I have also taken the trouble to learn the phrase *Fay chong chow*, which means 'very small', so when the day manager pours the Sprite and we talk about their honour and our honour, I point to my little map and intone, 'Ireland *fay chong chow,*' and then, stretching my arms wide, I smile, '... and China very big'. It works a treat. We do a deal to get the two snakes for the equivalent of £2 apiece.

I am even more cheered later in the day when I am introduced to Kenny Bloom. He is a wisecracking New York Jew and he is the first western record producer to hit Beijing. His reasoning was clear: 'When the accountants started making artistic decisions in New York, I knew it was time to get out and China seemed like a challenging place.'

Kenny quickly discovered how to tweak the system. Each album he recorded was under the aegis of a different ministry of the government. The ministries knew that something important was happening, even if they weren't quite sure what it was. Within a few months of arriving,

Kenny had set up a pop radio station and their first broadcast was listened to by 20 million people. By the second week the audience had grown to 100 million! Kenny now lives on the twenty-third floor of the New World building, a luxurious apartment block that towers over the teeming masses below, who are cooking their evening meal on the roadside to escape the stifling heat of their tenement homes.

The rest of the day is spent rounding up other guests for our Friday night show. Chen Da Men, a lively young man from CCTV, gets us a pop video producer, Xiao Chow Peng, and our own list includes Li An Min from Citic, Jim Dornan, our Coca Cola man, our popstar Wei Wei, our 'fixer' Tim Dyson, our American record producer, Kenny Bloom, our Scottish newspaperman, Ron Kidd (who hasn't yet repaid us our $300) and his fiancée, Xia Jiu. We also have a rebel newsreader-cum-rockstar called Wei Hua. She has been very outspoken since the massacre and is very unpopular with the authorities. We like rebels.

Friday morning dawns and still we have no equipment. We have been warned constantly that the secret police have us bugged, and at this stage I am so exasperated that I lean down to the bedside lamp in my room and say, 'For fuck's sake lads, would you give us our bleedin' gear.'

I scoot across to Li An Min. He seems to be the most powerful person we have met so far and asking him to be on the show has appealed to his preening vanity. Ostensibly I am meeting him to preview his questions for his interview, but in reality I believe he is our best hope of springing the equipment. It is a very instructional meeting.

He tells me disdainfully that our English 'fixer', Tim Dyson, is a small-time hustler and says that our interpreter, Pei Siu, is a no-hoper unless she gets herself better contacts.

My visit to Li An Min is in vain. The gear will not be released in time for tonight. A series of embarrassing phone calls are made and we decide to go and dine at the Ren Ren anyway. The Mayor of Beijing and CCTV have shown up for the occasion, so Wei Wei sings a few songs. In response, I sing 'Whole Lotta Shakin' Going On', 'Blue Suede Shoes' and 'Danny Boy'. They clap politely and Kenny Bloom takes great pleasure in telling me that I am wasting my time singing anything by Elvis.

'Nobody in China knows who the hell Elvis Presley is.'

Because the manager of the Ren Ren is angry and disappointed and in no mood to trust us to reschedule the filming, conniving Irishmen that we are, we have Pei Siu take us on to another restaurant, the Ju Ya. Pei Siu seems to be getting the hang of our shambolic style and miraculously we talk the manager into allowing us film 'Nighthawks in Beijing' on his premises the following Tuesday. Much celebratory drink is consumed.

Saturday morning starts with one mighty hangover, but the pain becomes bearable with the arrival, at last, of our equipment. We go to Zheng Chen Park, to the theatre where Wei Wei is performing for the Construction Workers. The theatre is dowdy and drab. Wei Wei sings three songs to the accompaniment of backing tracks. The rest of the show consists of a comedian, a magician, dancers and a mime artist. The audience is polite rather than exuberant. With only one camera, Declan and Liam have a furious amount of running around to do, but we're thrilled to be finally getting some footage in the can.

When I can grab the time in between shooting, I luxuriate in taking a taxi downtown and wandering around the shops on my own. In most places I am the only westerner on view and my big nose is getting plenty of attention. The Chinese disparagingly call westerners *Da wai dabiza* – big nose foreigners. Most curious of all, in my wanderings, are the *hutongs*, the small alleys that spread out in all directions. People seem to live in the smallest of cubby holes, one on top of another. I am charmed and fascinated, but I have to remind myself how easy it is to romanticise other people's poverty.

We take our camera to Wei Wei's home, which to our eyes looks like a run-down apartment block. But she is well off by Chinese standards. She sells about one million albums every year and because she is a public figure, she is allowed extra privileges. One perk, which Wei Wei enjoys enormously, is a small Jeep she has bought for her father.

Inside the family apartment, we meet Wei Wei's mother, father and brother. There are only two bedrooms and the living room is an all-purpose sitting room, dining room and bedroom. They have the luxuries of a fridge and a television, but the galley kitchen is narrow, dark and very pokey. The chemical toilet is out of order and this is bad news, as I am getting the call. Wei Wei's father directs me to the local market, which is just around the corner. I hurry around and the public toilet is a sight to behold. An open latrine runs the length of a twenty-foot wall. There are two small porcelain squat toilets. Otherwise it's down on your hunkers and use the pit, and woe to him that loses his balance. Once I am squatting, I am a stationary target. The flies are most inquisitive and so are the locals, especially the wide-eyed kids. As an entertainer, I've played to smaller audiences.

Later that night, Ron Kidd (who still hasn't even mentioned the $300) smuggles Declan, Liam and I into his living quarters inside the *People's Daily* compound. His flat is close to squalor. Ugly, damp walls, cracked sinks and naked light bulbs give it the feel of a gulag and we film it on a small, easily-concealed, non-professional video camera. Why we are here is beyond me. It seems like we are unnecessarily jeopardising our whole visit, but there is a great buzz from tasting the forbidden fruit.

Thankfully, on Tuesday a big crowd shows up for our rearranged 'Nighthawks'. Pei Siu is playing opposite me in three little snatches of soap opera, where I am pretending to be opening a branch of Nighthawks in Beijing. She is dressed up in a gold kimono and looks very attractive. The crowd is spudded with our ally from the Irish embassy, Eamonn Robinson, and all the other Irish and English expats. It is further swelled by the presence of a sizeable number of secret police. They are doing their best to be invisible and it is amusing to watch them trying to lean back in their chairs to see if they can overhear what my guests are saying. But the excitement of the occasion seems to be too much even for them, and at one point, two of them rise to offer me a cigarette.

However, the secret police are not entirely benign and I

am informed that once I am finished with them, my Chinese interviewees are being taken to the kitchen and interrogated. Ron Kidd (not a word about the $300) is most perturbed and very anxious about his fiancée, Xia Jiu.

A row breaks out between us and the manager when Wei Wei refuses to sing live. She is angry that she had been filmed during our failed attempt a few days earlier and the footage had been used on the news without her permission. She sticks to her guns and I have to produce my little map once more and do the *fay chong chow* shuffle one more time to get us out of an unseemly wrangle. Incredibly, the total bill for food and drink in the Ju Ya barely comes to a bit over two hundred pounds. The sight of money soothes the angry proprietor and we skedaddle before any more trouble erupts.

Declan, Liam and myself are totally elated. From a technical and production point of view, the two of them have done a job that is usually done by three times that number of people. But much more satisfying is the feeling that we have pulled off one of the great coups, scams or whatever you want to call it. Without any help from our supposed fixer, Tim Dyson, just a year after the Tiananamen Square massacre, we have flim-flammed our way past the paranoid authorities and produced a programme unlike anything that has ever come out of China up to that moment. To celebrate, we do the decent thing and get rat-arsed drunk.

But the drama isn't over. Next day, Ron Kidd (where is our $300?) and Xia Jiu get a tip-off from an unspecified embassy that the secret police are about to come for them.

We replay their interview in Liam's room and, falling back on our old ploy of conversing in Irish, Declan, Liam and I decide to erase a couple of contentious minutes. We also erase the footage we have shot of Ron's apartment in the *People's Daily* compound.

Ron and Xia Jiu are waiting anxiously in Tim Dyson's room and when we get there, we put our fingers to our lips to warn them to remain silent in case the room is bugged. I hand them a note I have written, explaining the action we have taken. They read the note and smile with relief. And then in a moment of high drama, or is it farce, I solemnly burn the note over the toilet and flush away the evidence.

Over the next few days we film Wei Wei's master interview. We follow her to the recording studios and after that we bring her out on the street and film people reacting to her. For one glorious hour, we manage to shake off Mr Ma, our hitherto constant companion, and Pei Siu takes us to an extraordinary market, full of exotic foodstuffs, trinkets and old men with long, grey, wispy beards, sitting on the pavement, selling a bewildering variety of birds in ornate cages.

Suddenly, out of nowhere, a young man in a crisp white shirt approaches us aggressively. 'You have permission?' he demands angrily. It is immediately apparent that he is no more than an officious young supporter of the regime, taking it upon himself to quiz the foreigners. 'Wei Wei,' I say, pointing at our pop star. 'Ah! Wei Wei.' Now he has a big smile and he is pumping Wei Wei's hand excitedly. There are star-fuckers everywhere, even in communist China.

Later in the day, on our way to the Great Wall, we get

the news that Madam Jiang and her friends from the Ministry of Culture want to view all the tapes we have shot. We discuss the ramifications *as Gaeilge* amongst ourselves, but the need for continued subterfuge vanishes when we reach the Great Wall. Mr Ma has obviously been up on the Great Wall one too many times and allows us to ascend unaccompanied.

Everyone knows what the Great Wall looks like, snaking its way up hills and down valleys, running off into the distance as far as the eye can see. This is a new section of the wall that has just opened to the public and it is not yet very busy. At one point I look to my right and I swear my breath is taken away when I realise that the only people I can actually see on the Great Wall are Declan, Liam and me. The Irish own the Great Wall. It feels like we've earned it.

It's a wrap. We have shot enough of Wei Wei to assemble a half-hour easily and I have been filmed goofing around and riding a bike in the midst of the mayhem, as inserts for our 'Nighthawks' programme. We have a celebratory dinner and we even forgive Tim Dyson for being useless. Then we are taken by our American friend, Kenny Bloom, to another unlikely destination. We pull up to a bar called Big Ben. As the door opens, the improbable strains of Branford Marsalis on saxophone come wafting out into the night air. Inside is a big square room, with moody lighting, casual seating, a small dance floor and a long bar. Along the bar are a bevy of beautiful young hookers. They are all smiles and not at all pushy. We talk to them and find out that most of them work in laboratories during the day.

'That's Communism for ya!' Kenny wisecracks. 'I'm a rocket scientist by day and I give blowjobs at night.'

Over in a corner, two young men and a girl are singing 'Stand By Me' to the accompaniment of an acoustic guitar. I go and stand beside them, listening, and when they finish, I applaud. 'Do another one,' I urge them. They only know the one song, so they do it again and this time I join in. When they finish, the young man who is playing the guitar sticks it into my hand.

'Play,' he says, not knowing that I am a man who needs little encouragement. I grab the guitar and launch into 'All Shook Up'. In that second, Branford Marsalis is turned down and the whole bar comes alive, with everybody out of their seats, dancing. It is like a scene from one of those silly Elvis movies, but I am loving it. This is the only kind of international language I am any good at. I catch Kenny Bloom's eye and I shout at him, 'So much for them not knowing Elvis!'

Madam Jiang arrives early next day to view the tapes. She is accompanied by Yang Me, Mr Jian and the ubiquitous Mr Ma. Pei Siu is tense and worried that her little bits of soap opera in our 'Nighthawks' programme will bring the wrath of officialdom down upon her. Up to this point, Madam Jiang has been feigning her understanding of English. Now she hangs on every word. Everything is okay until we reach our interview with the rebellious newsreader-cum-rockstar, Wei Hua. We have no choice but to erase it. We manage to spool past the bits of soap opera with Pei Siu and there are no further hiccups. And when everything has been viewed, they solemnly count the number of tapes, twice over.

The ever-supportive Eamonn Robinson and the gang at the Irish Embassy throw a farewell party for us. Sadly, because of official government policy, neither Wei Wei or Pei Siu are allowed to enter foreign embassies, but all the other friends we have made during our stay show up. We drink Pei Siu and Wei Wei's share, as well as our own, and on our way home the heavens open and a downpour of warm rain drenches us to the skin as we dance our way back to our hotel.

The great adventure is almost over. In spite of sore heads, everybody who had been at the party seems to be swarming around the hotel. There are kisses and hugs all around and then we head for the airport. Pei Siu professes herself sad to see us go and inside the terminal, as we approach the departure gate, Declan, Liam and I pull out all our Chinese money and present it to Pei Siu. She smiles in gratitude and then with a last embrace, we are on our way.

Just as I am about to pass through the gate, she calls out my name. I turn back to her. She looks at me with urgent intensity.

'I just want you to know … I am not like the rest of them.'

Postscript: Wei Wei was never allowed out of China. My friend Richard, who had set up our adventure, had fallen hopelessly in love with Wei Wei and for three fruitless years he tried to get her out of China and failed. He finally lost heart and his love withered on the vine. Wei Wei is still in Beijing. She married a fifty-five-year-old Swedish record producer, Michael Smith, and she is now the mother of three children. Tim Dyson died a couple of years ago; Richard moved to Florida and I have never discovered what happened to Pei Siu.

And Ron Kidd never gave us back our $300.

Chapter 27

STAND BY YOUR BATH

There are very few people who can claim to have sat in Tammy Wynette's bath and sung 'Stand By Your Man'. In all probability there were just the two of us: Tammy and me. And Tammy's dead now. So that leaves just one. Me.

This splashy moment happened in Tammy's house on Franklin Road, in Nashville, Tennessee. Tammy was known as the First Lady of Country and as we drove up to the house, we saw that the electronic wrought-iron gates had the name First Lady Acres fashioned in iron script across the expanse of the two gates.

But let me take you back a bit. The music business is crazy. A song can be dead for twenty years and suddenly somebody has a hit with it and the mad dance begins again for the songwriter. Sometimes it is an artist who falls from favour only to have some loony DJ deciding on a whim to play their record again, triggering a revival. And sometimes it is a producer whose touch goes cold for years, until somebody hip deems him to be cool again and he is back in the hunt. It was a combination of all these things that brought me into the orbit of Tammy.

Long ago, when Bill Martin and Phil Coulter were one of the hottest songwriting and publishing teams in British music, my friend Richard Gillinson worked for them at Mews Music, which had very swanky eleventh-floor offices in Alembic House on the banks of the Thames, in London. Martin and Coulter wrote two of the great mainstream tracks of all time, 'Puppet on a String' and 'Congratulations', big hits for Sandie Shaw and Cliff Richard respectively.

Phil Coulter was Billy Connolly's producer and Billy had sung three of my songs on various albums, so I was always welcome at Alembic House. And invariably, it would be myself and Richard Gillinson who would sit chewing the fat. Time passed and so did Mews Music, but Richard started his own company, and with a crusader's zeal, he called it Lionheart Music. Part of his crusade brought him to Nashville, where he became friends with a producer called Paul Richey, who was, once upon a time, manager of the country legend George 'No Show' Jones, who got his name for being unreliable.

Paul's brother, George, a well respected producer, piano player and songwriter, is married to Tammy Wynette, who used to be married to George Jones! See how the story is starting to mesh.

Tammy's career is in the doldrums in America, so next thing, my friend Richard Gillinson suggests to her husband, George Richey, that Richard should represent Tammy in the UK. It is a shrewd move. Richard is working on the basis that in 1975, on its *fifth* re-release, 'Stand By Your Man' had been a UK No. 1 and she had followed it up with another hit, the famous 'D.I.V.O.R.C.E.'. Then, under the tutelage of Phil Coulter, Billy Connolly (see the mesh again) had had a No.1 with his parody of 'D.I.V.O.R.C.E.', called 'D.O.G.'. On the back of that, Tammy went through another revival and soon had two best-selling compilations in the UK charts and the profile to go with it.

The notion of having another crack at Britain and Ireland was a great move for Tammy. My friend Richard put her together with a hot band of the time, KLF, and they had a hit in 1991 with a song called 'Justified and Ancient'. Tammy was hot again and that meant she needed to be in Britain. So one thing led to another and before you know it, myself and Richard are talking about making a documentary with Tammy.

I pitch the idea of a Tammy documentary to RTÉ television and they give me the money. With my director, Declan Farrell, we hatch a plan. Tammy is going to be in London. At ferocious expense, we reserve the penthouse suite in the Royal Garden Hotel in Kensington, fly our own crew to London and, trembling with anticipation, wait for the appointed moment for the big interview.

A worried-looking Richard approaches.

'Tammy isn't well. Her throat is really bad and we may not be able to do the interview.'

Holy shit! After all that expense.

'We'll give it a while and see how it goes.'

So we give it a while. And then more while. And even more while.

'Tammy has had the doctor and I'm really sorry but it's not going to happen today.'

Oh no!

'But, as compensation, she says if you want to, you can

come and do the interview in her house in Nashville.'

Oh yes!

We are buzzing by the time we drive up to First Lady Acres and see the gates swing open before us. It is really happening. George Richey, Tammy's husband, is the soul of graciousness and welcomes us warmly. He informs us that Tammy is having her hair and make-up done, so she will be a while. In the meantime, we are to have a look around and see what we'd like to film.

'Great house,' I say. 'Yes, its a nice house,' agrees George. 'It has fifteen bathrooms.' There is no answer to that.

George disappears and we start to poke around. The house is spacious and tasteful beyond our expectations. It is remarkably free of gee-gaws and country kitsch and Tammy has good taste in Chinese furniture. We take up George's challenge and, yee haw, we count them and it does indeed have fifteen bathrooms, including Tammy's de luxe miniature swimming pool. It is a big, fat, oval marble tub, about six feet long by four feet deep, with a foot-wide surround decorated with an extraordinary array of objects. It has two eighteen-inch gilt cherubs playing pan pipes, two twelve-inch tall oriental figurines, a gold locker, a marble-on-gilt wash stand, gilt taps, a gilt ashtray. And some greenery. This bath suits Tammy, down to the last bubble.

The walls of the halls are filled with gold discs from Tammy's long and successful career, but fools that we are, we first set up our camera in the very big kitchen. We have learnt nothing from our initial encounter with Tammy in

London. We wait five hours before Tammy is comfortable that her hair and make-up are perfect enough for the camera.

When she does appear, Tammy looks really well. Her make-up artist and one of her daughters are there for support. She is warm and welcoming. My nerves disappear as we launch into Tammy's life story and she is a total pro. She has been over this ground many times before, but you would never suspect it. She tells her story candidly, colourfully and with great freshness.

Tammy's real name was Virginia Pugh and she was born not far from Tupelo, Mississippi, where Elvis was born. Her father died when she was only ten months old. She was raised by her mother and grandmother and from an early age she picked cotton in the fields.

'Part of our land was in Mississippi and part in Alabama. I used to daydream about being a singer when I was out picking cotton in the fields.'

She married Euple Byrd when she is seventeen. He doesn't share her passion for music, so with three kids in tow, she moves to Nashville. She gets her break with a producer named Billy Sherrill, who was later to co-write 'Stand By Your Man' with her. She has two big hits with 'Apartment No. 9' and 'I Don't want To Play House'. Soon she has her first major hit with 'D.I.V.O.R.C.E.'.

But life is soon imitating art and Tammy's second marriage to guitarist Don Chapel begins to crumble when she finds out he's been selling nude pictures of her. Riding to the rescue comes one of the great characters of country music, George Jones, who wins her hand in a scenario as corny as a country song.

'I had been on the road workin' with Jones ... and I had three children and I arrived home and the kids were in hospital with food poison. Well, that night I couldn't find my husband Don and I needed help at the hospital. The only one I could think of was Jones. Next day I went home and I was sittin' at the table payin' bills and Don had come in and I wasn't very pleased with where he had been the night before ... and there was a knock at the door and it was Jones ... and Don said, "What is he doin' here?" ... and I said he was helpin' me last night with the kids. Don and I proceeded to fight and he was drinkin' some ... and he said some very unkind things about me ... usin' four-letter words ... and Jones said, "Don't talk about her like that" ... and Don said, "Why?" ... and Jones said, "Because I love her". He was grippin' the end of my table ... and he turned the table over ... destroyed my dining-room ... threw a chair through a plate glass window... and then he comes around and stood behind the chair I was sittin' on. He puts his hands on my shoulders and he says, "And she loves me too". I said, "Yeah" ... and he said, "Let's go"... and we left and I never went back.'

At the start, George Jones and Tammy Wynette are a marriage made in country heaven. George and Tammy record slushy, over-the-top romantic ballads, the most famous of which is 'The Ceremony', which is the marriage vows set to music. But inevitably the icing begins to melt on the cake and George becomes as famous for his drinking as he is for his singing. The great story they tell is that Tammy hid the keys to all of their cars so that George couldn't go to town to drink while she was out on an errand. She was hardly gone when George was spotted driving into town on the lawnmower!

Tammy's fourth marriage, to real estate agent Michael Tomlin, lasts just forty-four days. She follows that with a sensational affair with film star Burt Reynolds, but she finally finds a bit of stability with George Richey, the man who has now affably welcomed us into his house. George is all gold watches, gold necklaces and gold chains. His crowning glory is a humongous gold ring, which has an inset of piano keys, with a small diamond that dances up and down the notes as he moves his fingers.

But if Tammy has trouble with men, it is nothing compared to the health problems she has suffered. They started after the birth of her daughter Georgette, when she had an emergency appendectomy from which she suffered adhesions. The adhesions recurred and recurred, requiring further surgery each time.

'Between that and other operations, all in all, I've had seventeen major operations on my stomach.'

All the surgery and all the pain that went with it was a slippery slope for Tammy and she became addicted to painkillers. She eventually had to go to the famous Betty Ford Clinic to clean up her act.

'I was never actually detoxed, but they took me offa everything that I was taking. I stayed there for three weeks and then I collapsed and had to have surgery ... and the very thing that put me in there raised its head again. I had one more operation after that two years ago, and it's been great ever since.'

Hearing Tammy talk about her health raised the hare that maybe in London, when we were first supposed to interview her, Tammy had been having one of her anxiety attacks. In the aftermath of making the documentary, each time I got close to her in the subsequent months, she had health problems. It seemed like she could hardly pass through an airport without having to summon the doctor on duty. The last time I saw her was just before she performed in Dublin in 1996. She didn't look well.

In April 1998, Tammy was found dead, on the very same couch where she had sat when I interviewed her. The first reports said she had died in her sleep and that the official cause of death was heart failure. But the family was unhappy and, against George Richey's wishes, she was exhumed. The autopsy gave them no new information. At fifty-five years of age, the First Lady of Country Music was dead.

But let me take you back to when Tammy was still alive. As soon as I'd finished my interview for the documentary, she excused herself. Tammy and the band were setting off on tour that very night in her two big luxury coaches – Tammy 1 and Tammy 2. As she bade us goodbye, she left us in the hands of the housekeeper.

'You can film anything you want,' she said. 'Jest don't make a mess.'

We watch the red tail-lights of the two coaches glide down the driveway and out through the wrought-iron gates.

'She did say we could film anything, didn't she?' I query.

'Yes, she did,' agrees Declan.

'Follow me.'

I lead the way down the corridor to Tammy's super-duper bathroom. I turn on the taps and as the bath fills with water, I pour in a liberal helping of bubble bath. In no time at all, a souffle of bubbles has blossomed in the bath. I quickly slip off my shirt, then my pants and then my jocks. Stark naked, I immerse myself in the warm water, let my head rest against the taps and open my throat, embarking on a course of action that has ultimately marked me apart, as the only surviving human who has sung 'Stand By Your Man' in Tammy Wynette's bath.

Chapter 28

TEXAS TALES

To use the language of the trail, I have had a hankering to be a cowboy ever since I was a kid going to the Saturday matinees at the Ritz Cinema in Ballsbridge. Driving great herds of cattle across the plains seemed like the ultimate career choice, and riding bucking broncos and hog-tying steers looked like as much fun as anyone could have, while still calling it work. And then there was the camaraderie of the campfire at night, underneath the stars, with songs to be sung, beans to be eaten and stories of great cattle drives to be retold.

My first sight of Texas doesn't disappoint. It looks like cowboy country, vast and flat in all directions, with a big sky. Just like I imagined. The heat is dry and intense. All the men, from the hotel concierge to the panhandler in the street, sound like cowboys. I feel really at home.

We are in Austin, a low-slung city with a good musical pedigree. We are here to film a local musical legend, Butch Hancock. In Texas, they have their own brand of country and they enjoy bucking the trend of the powerful commercial record companies in Nashville. Renegades like Joe Ely and Guy Clark command extra respect, because they have made it in Nashville on their own terms. But the man who gets more respect than any other is Butch Hancock. The musos in Austin still talk with reverence of the three-night concert stint Hancock once did, where he never repeated a single song over the three nights.

Butch Hancock was born in Lubbock, Texas, the same town that gave us Buddy Holly. When we catch up with Butch in Austin, he is running an art gallery called Lubbock Or Leave It. If he lived in Europe, Hancock would be known as a renaissance man. He is a painter, a poet, a songwriter, an actor, a director, a photographer, an architect and a cartoonist.

One of the best bits of madness on display in his gallery is his Popcorn World cartoons. Combining his architectural training with his cartooning ability, Butch has created a world where people live inside giant bits of popcorn. The mad shapes of popcorn, the way they are knobbly and irregular, is offset by smoothing out the insides and skillfully adapting the shape to the individual needs of the occupants. It is a novel idea that is quite bonkers and is never going to happen. But it does highlight Butch's playfulness.

Another exhibit on display is a polystyrene cup about the size of a shot glass. Butch has a friend in the US navy who dives to great depths in his submarine. Sometimes he hangs a polystyrene cup attached to a string over the side for Butch and when the submarine descends to the depths, the pressure down deep shrinks the cup to the size of a shot glass. Butch enjoys showing them to people. How could you not like a man with such a fine sense of priorities?

The interview with Butch is very enjoyable. He is immensely likeable and without a trace of ego. When our chat is over and we are about to depart, I turn to Butch.

'Butch, whatever you do, promise me you'll keep pushing out those boundaries and looking for new things to do.'

With a great grin on his face, he drawls, 'When I was a young man, a friend of my father took me aside and said, "Son, go out there and don't spread yourself too thin." And I thought "spreading yourself thin" sounded like a great concept, so I've been doin' it ever since.'

After meeting Butch, I am ready for Texas with a vengeance. And I especially want to meet some real cowboys. We head out across the flat landscape to a very small town called Stonewall. Today is rodeo day. An arena built of scaffolding sits on the edge of town. All the pomp and panoply of a full-size rodeo is on display, even though it is all just a tiny bit shabby.

The rodeo begins with the arrival of a troop of kids and cowboys on horseback, dressed in the uniforms of the US Cavalry. They gallop into the ring, bugles blowing, banners flying and ride around the arena at speed until they eventually come to a halt before the VIP platform in the stand, which is filled by all the local dignatories.

The preacher intones a prayer. The cowboys stand, heads bowed and with their hats on their chests. The majority of them are Mexican ranch hands, brown and durable. Even the clowns have their heads bowed. The band plays 'God Bless America' and as I drink in the spectacle, my mind wanders back to the Saturday matinees in the cinema and to my hero, Roy Rogers.

Roy Rogers was known as the King of the Cowboys. In the Forties and Fifties, Roy made over ninety movies and a hundred television shows and became the biggest B-movie star in America. At the zenith of his popularity, there were over 2,000 Roy Rogers fan clubs all over America.

Roy was born in a place called Duck Run, Arkansas, and he grew up on a farm, hunting coons, fishing and doing all the chores that the farm demanded. During the Great American Depression in the 1930s, the family moved to California and Roy and his dad made a living as shoemakers, specialising in cowboy boots. Roy won a talent contest as a singer and he made his bid for movie stardom when, one day, he sneaked on to the studio lot and was spotted by a friend, who told him that the producers were looking for a singing cowboy. Roy was in the right place at the right time and his life was changed forever.

Although he could ride a horse and shoot straight, Roy was a cod cowboy. In his movies, he stood for integrity and Mom's apple pie. He rode a beautiful palomino horse called Trigger and had a trusty German Shepherd dog called Bullet. His movies were western parables, in which the good guys always triumphed over the bad guys. And Roy always got the girl.

With his backing group, the Sons of the Pioneers, Roy made many hit records. In his movies, the songs were big, elaborate set pieces, which required sophisticated staging. His voice was really pleasant and when he married his dueting partner and female lead, Dale Evans, together they came to represent all that was good and right about America.

Not everybody was fond of the singing cowboy genre of movies. There was a joke we used to tell about Roy:

'Roy! Them darn Injuns have gone wild an' burnt yer ranch tuh the ground. They've murdered yer kids ... an' they've raped yer precious wife, Dale.'

'Those varmints,' spits Roy. 'Why, I'll hunt them down, each an' every one ... an' chase 'em all the way to the Rio Grande if I have to ... but first a song.'

Roy Rogers was part of my childhood. I loved him as a movie hero, but I had forgotten about him until one day in 1992, I walk into Pat Henry's gym on Dublin's Pembroke Street. On the wall I see a picture of Pat standing beside Roy Rogers. I find out that Pat is a rabid Roy Rogers fan and has met the great man. I do some research with Pat and then I pitch the idea of a documentary on Roy to RTÉ Television. Just weeks later, Pat Henry is at the wheel of a Cadillac El Dorado, driving me, my director, Declan Farrell, our cameraman, Dave Burke, and our sound man, Piaras MacCionnaith, to Victorville in California, about four hundred miles from Los Angeles.

At that time, Victorville was the location of the Roy Rogers and Dale Evans Museum, an impressive wooden stockade fort standing on its own couple of acres, surrounded by flat, scrubby land that looks arid and unyielding. This is what the California High Desert looks like.

Outside the front gate of the fort, rearing up on his hind legs, is a massive thirty-foot-high statue of Roy's golden palomino horse, Trigger.

In a flurry of dust, and in full cowboy costume, Roy arrives to meet us. But it isn't dust that is raised by a horse's hooves. Even though he is seventy-nine, Roy is riding a big, powerful Honda 750cc motorbike. I climb on the pillion and, firing one of Roy's six-guns into the air, I whoop and holler as he takes me for a spin around the fort, circling the building three times. I relish the moment and think about the many guys who would give their eye teeth to be the pillion passenger behind the King of the Cowboys.

The museum attracts people from all over America and abroad. In his heyday, Roy's fans were mostly God-fearing good folk. A lot of them still are; folks who hanker for the old ways, when, just like the movies, things were black and white.

'In my movies, the good guys had white hats and the bad guys had black hats,' says Roy. 'And when you were having a fight, you had to hold on to your hat with one hand, 'cos if it got knocked off it could mess up the continuity on the next scene.'

Like the heroes of his movies, Roy in real life expresses his great respect for his flag and his country. He enjoys having the museum and being there isn't a chore to him. 'Every day,' Roy tells me, 'I put on muh hat and muh boots and I come down here and I am Roy Rogers for the folks.'

His daily pilgrimage to the museum also allows Roy to salute his faithful animal pals, Trigger and Bullet. In a glass case, Trigger is beautifully stuffed and mounted on his hind legs in a rearing position. Below Trigger sits Bullet, his long, stuffed tongue flopping out over his teeth.

'They're talking about stuffin' me some day too,' laughs Roy.

The rest of the display cases contain hundreds of posters, photographs and costumes from his movies. In his films, Roy wore a snazzy line in colourful cowboy shirts, bedizened with rhinestones. There is also a collection of antique farm machinery, saddles, guns and cars. Roy's favourite car is an open-top Caddy with a six-gun motif. The door handles are in the shape of six-guns. So is the gearshift. There are six-guns on every surface – on light switches, on the handbrake, on the window handles. Even on the ashtrays.

Dale Evans comes bustling up to us, full of 'Praise the Lord'. As she leaves, I ask Roy how they get along after all their time together. 'Oh,' he says, his face a stoic mask, 'She does her thing and I do mine.'

In their younger years, Roy and Dale did a lot of humanitarian work. They also raised a diverse family of children. Roy's first wife Arlene gave birth to three children, Cheryl Darlene, Linda Lou and Roy Junior, who became known as Dusty. A week after Dusty's birth, Arlene died of an embolism and Roy was left a widower with, as he said himself, 'three young kids and thirty-four coon dogs'. But in true Hollywood fashion, Roy proposed to his screen partner Dale in the middle of an arena, in the middle of a show and Dale accepted.

Four years later Roy and Dale had a daughter, Robyn,

who was a Downs Syndrome child and she died just before her second birthday. Two years later, they adopted a Native American girl, Mary Little Doe, and the same year they adopted Sandy, another orphan, who was slightly brain-damaged. And they weren't finished yet. In 1955 they adopted a Korean orphan, Deborah Lee.

Sadly, Deborah lee was killed in a bus crash when she was twelve and Sandy died in his sleep shortly after he joined the army.

When I was leaving Victorville, Dusty gave me a copy of their family's 'Home Movies', which showed them doing typical family stuff like cavorting around the pool and sharing Christmas in what looked like a warm and loving atmosphere. I still have it and treasure it.

The Roy Rogers Museum has since moved to Branson, Missouri, but my last memory of Roy was when we shook hands and began to pull away. Roy waved his farewell and delivered his signature sign-off line, 'Happy trails to you'.

Three years later, a happy trail has brought me to the Cowboy Museum at 209 Alamo Plaza, San Antonio, Texas. The proprietor is a real cowboy. His name is Jack Glover and he is a slim and leathery seventy-year-old with a droopy moustache. America seems to have a penchant for old cowboys with museums.

'Were there any Irish cowboys?' I ask.

'Oh, sure. There were lots of Irish cowboys,' he twangs.

'And the strangest thing about them was that when they hadn't seen each other for a long time, the way they would greet each other was by punching each other out!'

In his younger life, Jack rode the trail and slept in bunkhouses on ranches all over Texas. I ask him how they passed the nights in the bunkhouse.

'Wa'al,' he says, 'those of us that could read would read – if we had a candle or a bit of oil. But a lot of them couldn't read, so sometimes a feller would pick up a can of beans and recite what was on the back for the rest of the fellers.'

When I am leaving, Jack calls me aside and hands me a book.

'I want yuh tuh have this.'

It's a sizeable paperback, bearing the title: *The 'Bobbed Wire' Bible*, VIII, by Jack Glover.

I flick through the pages and, mad as it may seem, they are filled with drawings of different kinds of barbed wire, or as they call it, 'bobbed wire'. The different varieties have exotic names: Scutt's Double Clip, patented by HB Scutt in 1880, and Haish's S Barb Hog Wire, patented 1876. Page after page, the drawings go on. And this is Volume Eight!

This book is probably the most exotic gift I have ever received. And listening to Jack and his stories has satisfied some of my longing to know the lore of cowboys. Ole Jack and I have become real buddies by now. We shake hands with the intensity of two men who know they will never meet again. I look at the flyleaf of the book and I see that he has written something on it.

'For friend Shay ... a great spirit, from old ornery Jack Glover'.

Chapter 29

RAY AND SHAY'S JAPAN

Izumo is a small town in the southwest of Japan. It is known as the Land of a Million Gods. The people of Izumo have been enterprising enough to offer themselves as hosts to the Irish international football team for the week immediately preceding the soccer World Cup in 2002. This shrewd move has galvanised the citizens of Izumo to create a publicity coup for their town, as well as giving them an active stake in the World Cup celebrations.

Whatever Ray Treacy has told them about me being a famous songwriter and television star in Ireland, it has had the desired effect and our Japanese hosts in Izumo greet us at the airport with a phalanx of flag wavers and cheering officials from City Hall.

We are driven to City Hall in the biggest car in town, to be greeted by the Mayor, Masahiro Nishi. There are three television crews and countless press looking for quotes, and between myself and Ray, we dole out a Mount Fuji-size ration of bullshit.

Ray Treacy is the travel agent for the Irish soccer team. He is also a former international centre-forward, fondly remembered by Irish fans for his bustling style and great prowess with his head. Ray and myself are fronting a TV programme called 'Ray and Shay's Japan' and our mission is to film the hotels the Irish team will be staying in, and the pitches they will be playing on, during the forthcoming World Cup. As well as being the co-presenter, I am also the director and my cameraman is Eamonn Taggart.

We check into our hotel, which is also to be the team hotel for the Irish squad during their week of preparation. Everywhere we go there are people to open doors and carry our bags. Ray and myself travel in the biggest car, which has white cloths, like doileys, draped over every seat. It looks very posh.

There are big welcoming signs around the town and the Irish tricolour waves proudly in front of many buildings. Mayor Nishi is a genial and jovial character who speaks good English, and his staff are most attentive. In fact, they are so attentive that everywhere we travel for the next thirty-six hours, we are accompanied by Sota San, Ichitobi San, Yota San, Kodama San, Okad San and several more. There are never less than twelve in our party, and trying to be a television director in the middle of all of that would be very intimidating if I didn't have such a hard neck. Instead I enjoy the comicality of it all, especially when Eamonn pans the camera suddenly, causing our flying wedge of a dozen to scurry out of the way.

We have a long lunch with the Deputy Mayor at a local winery. The smoked salmon, pumpkin soup and steaks are most enjoyable, but we have scarcely finished when we are told that the Mayor must fly to Tokyo tonight, so the official welcoming dinner will be at six-thirty. We've just finished lunch, for God's sake.

Dinner is in the poshest restaurant in town. We remove our shoes and are shown into a private dining room, which has a well hollowed out underneath a traditional Japanese table, to accommodate our occidental feet. The effect is that we look like we are sitting cross-legged in traditional style.

The dinner is unexceptional, but as we loosen up, a karaoke machine miraculously appears. I had assumed that I'd have to wait until I got to Tokyo before I would get to see and hear the much-vaunted Japanese karaoke and now here it is in the most sophisticated restaurant in Izumo. Nobody tries to duck out. Everybody in our official swarm takes a turn and even though some of them are diffident and shy, honour is at stake, especially when Treacy San and Healy San eschew the use of the machine and give them a rattle of 'The Fields of Athenry'.

Meantime, the Mayor has left for Tokyo, but, with a complete lack of pretension, his deputy does a good job of singing. And so too does the Chairman, a Mr Magoo look-alike, who as well as being chairman, is also a Shinto monk.

Our fixer in Japan is Declan Somers. He is a small, wiry leprechaun of a man from Carlow, with a sparkling intelligence and great humour to boot. I immediately take to him. He speaks flawless conversational Japanese, which he tells me he learnt in the most practical way. Having enrolled at Tokyo University, he realised that what they were teaching him in the classroom was useless. Instead he went to the student bar and learnt to speak real, everyday Japanese. His ease with the language and his personal charm will be invaluable to us over the coming days.

Declan takes us to the Shibuya section of Tokyo, where there is a statue to a famous dog, Hatchiko. This German shepherd accompanied his master, Professor Inurban Enuye, to the train every day and waited at the station till he returned each evening. In 1925, the Professor died, but for ten years afterwards, Hatchiko would still pad faithfully to the station and wait for his master. The people of Tokyo, touched by his loyalty, erected a statue to him.

We are expected at Paddy Foley's pub. And this is where the world does one of its famous shrinking tricks. The pub is owned by Mike Shannon, who is a son of Ken Shannon, my first camera crew leader when I joined RTÉ television as a cameraman in 1963. He was a sweet, laid-back, gentle character who nudged me forward with a smile and words of encouragement.

Michael is heavy-set compared to my memory of his razor-thin father. Ken died when he was only fifty-two, to be followed by his wife Patricia just a year later. Paddy Foley's pub is called after Mike's mother, Patricia Foley. Because of my connection with his father and mother, I realise it is important for Mike that I can give him more memories of his parents to fuel his store, so I am happy to oblige.

Next morning, myself and Eamonn walk across to investigate a shopping mall and along the way we find a flea market. I have often wondered why they are called flea markets. Is it because they are places where fleas sell to lesser fleas? This place has all the elements of old crap being sold on down the line, but I pick up some useful bargains in Zippo lighters and gunk like that. I also have a good time talking to stallholders with my hands, especially when it comes to buying music that I might find useful as a soundtrack for the shoot. I finally buy some secondhand CDs and I remedy my plight of not being able to listen to them by commandeering a boombox from one of the stallholders and listening to the CDs on the spot. One of the CDs is eminently right and I present the others as a thank-you to a delighted boombox owner.

Our next act is one of selfishness on my part. As night draws in, we get the front seat on a driverless monorail train that runs high above the city streets. Below us, cars – looking like Dinky toys – and antlike people scurry around as the train shimmies its way between the lit-up skyscrapers, like a helicopter snaking in and out of pools of sudden darkness, then hurtling around a bend headlong into the blaze of neon that is Tokyo. For me, who has always been in thrall to city lights, it is a trip in every sense of the word and the most alluring and satisfying part of our visit. Afterwards I feel like a vampire who has just gorged on a virginal neck.

Tonight is to be our night on the town. We don't have a big night, but it is certainly a beguiling one. We meet Mick Shannon in a small bar in the studenty, bohemian sector of Tokyo. Mick has cued up Thin Lizzy to be playing 'Don't Believe A Word' when we walk up the stairs to this tiny bar, which has just about enough room for twenty people. We sit along a bench at the bar, behind which are three funky young guys who cook for us, shake us our cocktails and are genial and warm.

We leave there, noting on the way that the prices for the Blow-Job Bar upstairs vary between 3,000 and 6,000 yen, depending on the hours you require your fellatio. Our man Declan tells us that, being foreigners, we are unwelcome to do anything more than look at the menu.

Next we wander down a shady side street. A revolving, coloured mushroom outside a door is the only evidence of activity within. This is an even smaller bar than the one we have just left.

This bar is the size of a large toilet. There are three people sitting on stools immediately inside the door. The room is so narrow that we have to squeeze behind them to reach the far end. Two more guys sit on the small part of the L-shaped bar. With the arrival of myself, Eamonn, Declan and Mick, the place is now technically full. And behind the counter is Puttin and his girfriend/manager.

Puttin is about six feet tall, with that strange, orangey-coloured hair that comes from trying to dye away the severe blackness of Japanese hair. He has a cheeky monkey style and he wears a tight skullcap. He sports a genial smile and, by all acounts, at one time he was a professional boxer. The Beatles are playing on the sound system. Puttin turns out to be a complete Beatles freak. He takes his guitar and sings 'Blackbird', playing it beautifully. And we can't help smiling when he mangles the English language in a flurry of 'brackbirds' taking lonely wings to learn to 'fry'.

And then it is our turn. We sing 'Will You Go, Lassie Go'

and everyone, well the whole eleven of us, love it. Then it is handshakes all around and a dash for the last train back to our hotel in Chiba.

My final Japanese musical encounter happens when we travel to Harajuka Park, where every Sunday an army of the most outrageous Goths, in their trademark black, gather outside the park entrance. Interspersed amongst the Goths are other young girls dressed as French maids, girls with ghoulish make-up dressed in doctors' white coats and one fantastic girl who is dressed as a PVC bird, with an extraordinary PVC beak. We get them to teach us Japanese phrases on-camera and Declan is brilliant at explaining to them exactly what we want.

We enter the park and a load of imitation Elvis hip-swivellers are dancing around a boombox playing rockabilly music. In another manifestation of Japanese exhibitionism, they dance for show, competing with each in their elaborate moves. For a laugh I jump in and begin to swivel my hips with the confidence of a man who has lived through the best days of Elvis.

The punters standing around are having a bit of a laugh at my antics, until this really big dancer in a black leather jacket, blue jeans and crepe-soled shoes, grabs me by the shoulder and with an inscrutable and implacable expression, frog-marches me to the periphery of his imaginary dance floor.

I look up at him with his big quiff and his long sideburns.

'D'ye know what it is?' I say. 'You're just jealous.'

Chapter 30

BIG ROSY

There is an ancient truism that is common to many cultures: 'If you want to make God smile, tell Him your plan'. At some point in our lives things happen to us all that make a mockery of our plans and all you can do is to try to roll with the situation and let it happen. A man trying to control his destiny might as well try to manipulate the tides, or turn back the night.

The Irish tenor, Ronan Tynan, was a qualified doctor when he won a talent contest called 'Go For It', on RTÉ television in 1994. He must have thought, not unreasonably, that this moment would be the turning point in his career. A life in music would surely open up before him and all his dreams of being a famous singer would come true.

But it didn't work out that way. He got a kick from a horse, which damaged his sinuses, and his singing suffered because of it. He concentrated instead on being a doctor and opened a clinic in his native Johnstown, County Kilkenny, where he treated people with bad backs. That's what he was doing when I met him.

Ronan is a truly remarkable character. When he was twenty-one he elected to have both his legs amputated from the knee down because of a deformity in both his ankles. This big, cheery, country lad with a beaming smile and sticky-out ears, exuded a zest for life that was so contagious that I asked him to be my guest on a television show called 'The Birthday Show'. He was as refreshing a guest as I hoped he might be, devoid of self-pity and optimistic about the future.

And this is where fate intervened. As film-makers, myself and my colleague Marion Cullen pitched a documentary idea to RTÉ for a series called 'Against the Odds'. Our story concerned an actor/writer who came from a background that was steeped in criminality, and his tale of art triumphing over ignorance was ideal for the series. But at the last minute our subject took the decision that being involved could possibly cause damage to his family.

Faced with this dilemma, we put on our thinking caps and I remembered Ronan. I rang him and asked him could we pitch his story. He agreed instantly, and in a matter of hours the story was written. RTÉ was happy with the substitution and Ronan's life was now about to take that quantum leap that had so cruelly evaded him after winning the talent contest.

I never told Ronan that he was our second choice for the documentary, or how close he had come to possibly being left in musical obscurity forever. He would undoubtedly have had a very satisfactory life helping people with back problems, but for him the documentary was a gift from the gods. On the strength of his voice and the success of the documentary, I got him a recording deal with Sony (Ireland) and he made his first album, 'My Life Belongs to

You', produced by his old school classmate, Frank McNamara. Suddenly, instead of manipulating discs, he was recording one. Suddenly, instead of talking to patients, he was talking to a camera.

Making the documentary was great fun. One might expect a man with two artificial legs to be cowed by life, but this genius was going at full speed. The first thing we found out was the depth of passion Ronan had for his horses. He rode out every day, but most remarkably he participated in show-jumping competitions, with a fearlessness that was breathtaking. He had show-jumping legs that were already in place in his jodhpurs, so all he had to do was pull them on and, with a minimum of fuss, he was ready to go.

Ronan was entered for a competition in the Dublin Horse Show. This was to be one of the strongest sequences in the documentary and anything could happen. Ronan was full of stories of the horse stopping at jumps and dumping him out of the saddle. On one occasion, he was catapulted over a wall and when two stretcher-bearers from the St John's Ambulance first aid crew ran to lift him up, one of them got the fright of his life when Ronan's false legs came away in his hands.

We assemble our crew at eight o'clock in the morning for the shoot. Ronan has told us that he will be jumping at nine. Something prompts me to head for the show-jumping arena earlier than planned and as we get closer, strolling at a leisurely pace, we suddenly hear the public address announcer say, 'Our next competitor, Number 284, is Ronan Tynan from Kilkenny'.

We take off at a run, camera and sound leads flying. We gallop as fast as we can to where Ronan is galloping as fast as he can. Our cameraperson, Deirdre Noonan, fires the camera up onto her shoulder and manages to get Ronan jumping his last obstacle and galloping through the finish. Now we are in trouble. We have blown our one shot at filming Ronan in a show-jumping competition.

But never say die. After a fulsome apology from Ronan for the mix-up, we put on our happy face and set about finding a solution. We bring Ronan into the practice ring and by dint of some judicious close-ups of flying hooves, close-ups of the horse's head and low-angle shots of Ronan jumping, we manage to simulate the action parts of his jumping round. Then we bang off close-ups of the 'Start' and 'Finish' signs, close-ups of officials, close-ups of spectators and we round it out with shots of the clock, the bunting and the various jumps. We pull off a little miracle and later, when our editor Paul Giles gets hold of the pictures, he cuts together a seamless sequence of a man on a galloping horse, that is so good that a man on a galloping horse wouldn't notice that it wasn't the real thing.

There is one other obstacle to overcome in making the documentary. How can we show that Ronan is a double-amputee without appearing too prurient? I know he is fond of swimming, so we hit on the idea of filming him swimming in a pool. He is totally unselfconscious as he walks to the edge of the pool and takes off his two pros-thetic legs. When he hits the water, the sight of the two artificial legs standing side-by-side on the pool's edge give us a dramatic illustration of the extent of his disability and how well he copes with it.

The documentary is called 'Dr Courageous' and it follows the path of Ronan's early life. He was highly motivated from the start and losing his legs only spurred him on to become the first double amputee to qualify as a Physical Fitness Instructor from Thomond College in Limerick. Then he went to the World Disability Games in New York and over the next couple of years he won eighteen gold medals and broke fourteen world records. But just when it seemed like he was set for a career in sports, Ronan changed tack and studied medicine. He was attached to the Meath Hospital as an intern when he won the 'Go For It' contest.

There was a huge response to the documentary and, with a record under his belt as well, more and more opportunities began opening up for Ronan as a professional singer. I could feel how torn he was between medicine and singing and I am happy to say I was one of the people to give him the nudge to abandon medicine and 'go for it'.

Ronan linked up with Wexford tenor John Kearns and the already established tenor Finbarr Wright, to form the Irish Tenors. A major television show for PBS in America was in the works. Ronan took to America like a duck to water. I knew Americans would love him for his indomitable spirit, his openness and his natural Irish charm. Before long he was giving motivational speeches as well as singing, and his larger-than-life personality was soon opening doors that had never been open to an Irish singer before.

He found a great admirer in George Steinbrenner, the

owner of the New York Yankees baseball team. Steinbrenner invited Ronan to throw the opening pitch of the 2001
World Series in Yankee Stadium. This is the kind of
honour that is reserved for very special Americans, yet
here, only a wet week in America, the gentle giant from
Johnstown was throwing the first pitch and singing 'God
Bless America' in one of the cathedrals of baseball.

In the aftermath of 9/11, Ronan became associated with
the firemen of New York and America began treating
Ronan as one of its favourite adopted sons. I laughed
when I heard that President Bush and his family had
become admirers and to date Ronan has sung for the Bush
Family six times. He was also asked by Nancy Reagan to
sing at the commemoration service for Ronald Reagan, and
after the funeral he was whisked off to Houston on the
Presidential jet, Airforce One, to sing for George Bush's
birthday the next day. It doesn't get much posher than
that. And he topped all his exploits by singing at the inau-
guration ceremony for George Bush's second term as
President.

Ronan is now a New Yorker as much as a Kilkenny man
and I see the sheer force of his personality at work up
close when I visit him in New York. We finish lunch and
Ronan invites me to come and see his new apartment.

'How far is it?' I query.

'About forty blocks,' he replies.

'Will we get a cab?'

'Would ya go 'way out of that! We'll walk.'

We set off walking up Third Avenue. The day is sunny
and his stride is long, Big Rosy, as they call him now,

throwing his legs out in front of him in the rolling gait he has developed to get the maximum from his prosthetic legs. Only once ever, in all the time I've known him, have I heard Ronan complain about his legs and when he did, it was just a small complaint: 'My stumps are killing me'. I was very familiar with the pains of a double amputee's stumps. My Da lost both legs five years before he died and I knew what he had been through. This first-hand experience was obviously part of the reason I was attracted to Ronan. Sadly, my Da never got to meet Ronan. They were cut from the same brave cloth and they would have got on like a house on fire.

At five feet eleven inches, Ronan dwarfs me as he pulls me up Manhattan in his slipstream. His bulk, coupled with his height, makes him very physically impressive, even though he once told me that sometimes, if he is feeling insecure, he will put on a pair of legs that give him an extra couple of inches in height. This day, however, there is no sign of insecurity and as we get closer to his apartment, a remarkable thing begins to happen. Shopkeepers begin to shout greetings to Ronan from their doorways. People walking dogs give him a cheery wave. Construction workers call him 'Big Guy'. Ronan has reduced New York to a village and turned it into Johnstown with yellow cabs.

Our progress gets slower and slower, as he gets more and more caught up in conversation with doormen, postmen and little old ladies walking poodles. When we reach his eyrie, he throws open the window and turns on the CD player. Loud. And then he begins to sing along with the Italian tenor, at full volume.

'Pardon me, Ronan,' I say. 'But what does the little old lady next door with the poodle have to say about this noise?'

'What can she say,' laughs Ronan. 'Have you seen the size of me?'

Chapter 31

WHAT'S JOHNNY LOGAN
DOING NOW?

Are you still with me? Great staying power. It's been a bit
of a rollercoaster ride, and the whole point of a rollercoaster ride is that you don't get a break: it keeps moving. So,
to keep this particular ride going I have left out some of
the bits – a bit of scaffolding here, an interesting bit of
scenery there. And, in case you missed them, here they
are:

This book might have been titled 'On the Boards' but for
a mishap early in my career. As a fourteen-year-old, I
appeared in a play alongside my mother and father in the
Damer Hall on St Stephen's Green in Dublin. The play was
an Irish-language translation of an Italian play by one Diego
Fabbri and the story concerned a bunch of wandering Jews
who decide to re-enact the trial of Jesus. They draw lots to
see who will play Herod, Peter, Caiphas and so on.

In the audience, there are three 'plants' – an actress/
prostitute, who is moved to give 'spontaneous' testimony
on behalf of Jesus; an actor/prodigal son, who also inter-
rupts unbidden; and me, a 'blind boy', sitting in the front
row. The play is a horrendous four-hour marathon and

even though my little speech is over and done before the end of Act 1, I have to return after the interval and sit through the whole of Act 2 in the front row. It's a tough gig for a teenager.

Each night we take the precaution of keeping the seats either side of me vacant or occupied by friends as a buffer against strangers becoming alarmed when I jump to my feet. One night, just before curtain-up, I break one of the lenses in my dark glasses. In a terrible panic, I hack a piece of cardboard from a box, colour it with black greasepaint and jam it into the wire frame of the glasses. I barely make it out front in time.

To my horror, just as the curtain rises, a posh-looking woman in a fur coat – a total stranger – sits in the seat right next to me. I am rigid with terror at this turn of events and then the unthinkable happens and the piece of coloured cardboard falls from the glasses and lands somewhere on my lap. I surreptitiously start to feel around with my hand without looking down and, after some unsuccessful fumbling, I sense from her discomfiture, that the woman beside me has come to the conclusion that I am 'fiddling' with myself.

In the normal run of the play I am supposed to stand up and cry out, *as Gaeilge*, 'I'm a blind boy'. At this point I am to twist my body to the left and face the audience. But the bit of cardboard is missing from the left side of the glasses so when my moment comes, I twist to the right instead. Pandemonium. Everybody in the cast is thrown and lines are missed, left, right and centre. At that moment, I am cured of my desire to be an actor.

But I was destined for showbiz in some form. As I was growing up, my mother taught me a whole raft of Irish ballads and when the folk boom happened in the 1960s, I was in the thick of it, singing and writing funny ballads and acting as emcee at concerts and folk clubs.

As well as being an active 'folkie', I also had one of the most glamourous jobs in Ireland – cameraman with RTÉ Television. I joined in 1963, when the station was just two years old. It was a hive of creativity and collective enthusiasm. We even drank with the accountants.

The cameraman's job was the one everybody wanted; looking through the lens at pop stars, dancers, actors and singers. I often compared us to fighter pilots, our hair blowing in the wind – even when there was no wind – swooping in and out with our cameras, performing dives and rolls, doing our own earthbound form of aerial ballet. A lot of the programmes we did were 'live' and I remember the tension and the potential for disaster as I forced my way through the crowd of studio dancers to get close-ups of Brendan Bowyer and the Royal Showband – kings of the Irish showband scene in the 1960s.

My most thrilling moment as a cameraman came the night we burnt the GPO in Studio 1. We were filming a programme called 'Insurrection' to celebrate the fiftieth anniversary of the Easter Rising of 1916, when a handful of Irishmen and women took on the might of the occupying

British Army. One of the leaders was Patrick Pearse and he was in command of the Irish Volunteers in the General Post Office, in the heart of Dublin.

The scene we are about to shoot calls for Pearse to walk back into the centre of a burning GPO, to take a last poignant look around before he presents the surrender. Tony Barry is the chief cameraman and he is sitting on a motorised camera called a crane, which will start its shot by looking back at Pearse from inside and slowly track back from the scene, pivoting around Pearse as it goes. The other three cameras, including mine, are poking through holes in the full size mock-up, picking up close-ups and shots of the flames.

As we get close to recording, the special effects man, who has come especially from England, daubs the set with a flammable gel. However, our director, Louis Lentin, is a bit of a martinet and a seeker after perfection, so the rehearsals drag on forever. When we finally get ready to film the scene, someone suggests that maybe the gel has dried out. More gel is applied.

The instruction, 'Light the set', is barked out. The flame touches the two coats of gel and with one big whooosh, a fierce conflagration is in full flame. The heat is instant. Tony Barry starts his long, slow backtrack. Eoghan Ó Súil-leabháin, the actor playing Pearse, walks into the centre of the set, wearing a thick serge army uniform. The flames are licking dangerously high and a pall of black smoke has bounced off the ceiling of the studio and has started back down again. We get all our shots and as we head, rapidly, for the exit, we can hear the shrill voice of our director shouting over the earphones, 'For Chrissake, stay on your cameras'. But none of us are prepared to die for Ireland behind a camera.

The lights are switched off. The security men usher everybody out of the studio. The hair on Eoghan Ó Súilleabháin's chest is singed, even through his thick uniform. And Tony Barry, who has magnificently shot this dramatic scene on the crane, is now minus eyelashes and eyebrows. The hare-brained notion has paid off and we are all still alive!

My other great moment as a cameraman came at the other end of the camera, so to speak. My birthday fell on Easter Sunday and I was working on a 'live' mass from Studio 2. I asked the director, Adrian Cronin, would it be all right for me to operate Camera 2 in the centre aisle, where I could lock-off my camera and leave him a static picture to cut away to as I went up to receive Holy Communion. When I arrived at the altar, my fellow cameraman on Camera 3 almost went down my gullet with his tightest lens and I received Holy Communion in the biggest close-up ever seen at any service of any denomination.

I changed sides of the camera in 1967 and hosted my first television show, 'Ballad Sheet'. I had a sub-Beatle haircut, I wore a lot of V-necked sweaters and all my intros were tightly scripted and dull. I followed that with 'Hootenanny' in 1969, a country music hoedown, which should have stayed down. And then in 1971, I was the presenter of a talent show, 'Reach For The Stars'. The show ran for thirteen weeks and for the final I wore a honey-brown velvet suit, which had a waisted jacket and flared trousers. When I moved the suit shimmered in the light. My matching bow tie was big enough to fly to America. The winner of the contest was Fran O'Toole, lead singer with the Miami Showband. He was a very sweet guy, who sadly, fours years later in 1975, along with two of his bandmates, Tony Geraghty and Brian McCoy, was shot and killed by the UVF on their way home from a gig in Banbridge, County Down, in a notorious incident remembered as the Miami Massacre.

Because there was no cable or satellite TV, television in 1971 was still a bit of a single-channel novelty and anyone who appeared on it became a major celebrity. I travelled the length and breadth of Ireland, singing my funny songs and telling my funny stories and in my own way, I was a star.

What happened next is a mystery. At the age of twenty-eight, I turned my back on a burgeoning television career in Ireland and went to live in America for four years. Looking back, I don't remember having a precise plan or any clear idea of what I was aiming for. I lived in Norwood, just outside Boston, for a year, then moved to Nashville for two years and finished my sojourn with a five-month stay in South Yarmouth, on Cape Cod, Massachusetts.

I loved America. I clicked with the audience there. They

liked me. And I liked them.

But, sadly, I had run foul of the immigration authorities. My papers had not been properly filed by my sponsor and after a running battle that went as far as trying to enlist the help of Senator Ted Kennedy, I had to admit defeat. I made a voluntary exit to avoid being deported and on 18 November 1975, I arrived back in Dublin with my wife and two children and so much baggage that the porter who was pushing our trolley looked at me and said, 'Why didn'tya get yer own plane?' I was home.

Just a week later I am back at Dublin Airport with a bunch of guys, to pick up the legendary manager of the Rolling Stones, Andrew Loog Oldham. We are having a drink in the Arrivals bar when a UDA (Ulster Defence Association) terrorist bomb explodes. When a bomb explodes, there is no loud bang. Instead you hear a thud, followed by a whoosh as the blast of air hits you. Without really feeling it happen, our party is blown to the ground. We are lucky. One poor unfortunate who is in the toilet backing onto the bar is killed. The bar and all its bottles are shattered in the blast, dripping their contents on to the floor, like a shot-up saloon scene from an old western movie. Mothers with children bleeding from cuts inflicted by flying shards of glass sit numb and dumbfounded. What I remember most is seeing the people who have been blown onto the floor, me included, trying to burrow under each other as we anticipate a second blast.

We are directed out by the security men. We duck behind the bar and get out to the car park. We have travelled out in a huge American car owned by a high-roller of the day, Aimen Cannon. On our way back into town, shock begins to set in and Andrew Oldham orders the driver, Simon Buckland, to pull over. He gets out of the car, opens the trunk and retrieves a leather Gladstone bag. He opens the bag and in it he has an extensive cornucopia, or perhaps it is a pharmacopia, of pills, powders and potions. He looks into each of our shocked faces and with the confidence of a trained diagnostician, he doles out a red pill here, a yellow tablet there and a blue one for the driver.

In 1978, John McColgan, my old friend from our days together in RTÉ as cameramen, brought me in as Publicity Officer for the new RTÉ 2 television service. I clicked in the job, but I had acquired an enemy high up on the sanctified, executive third floor in RTÉ.

This individual was not enamoured of my long hair and my loud clothes, so he aimed his metaphorical sniper's rifle at me on the pretext that RTÉ had publicly announced they were not taking on any new staff. But before he could pull the trigger, somone pointed out to him that because I was doing a good job, they would look foolish if they got rid of me.

Now they were in a quandary. They looked around to see if there was any kind of vacant position that might accommodate me, and lo and behold, the senior post of

Press & Information Executive had an empty chair. In one of those Jesuitical solutions so beloved of the organisation, I was appointed *Acting* Press & Information Executive but, unlike the previous tenant, I would not be a spokesman.That couldn't have suited me better. I had no desire to be consulted at four o'clock in the morning as to why the transmitter in the Sligo Mountains wasn't working.

I held on to my desk in RTÉ 2 and I now had an office in the main headquarters as well. I also had a staff of six women, who were technically my responsibility, so I went to them and explained that I knew nothing about overtime, days off, sick days and work schedules. I told them to carry on as before and to be practical and pragmatic in self-regulating their schedules. And lastly, I instructed them that if anyone rang looking for me, they were always to say that I was en route from RTÉ 2.

Then, on 19 April 1980, my ship came in. The BIG break I was chasing walked in through my door and I carved myself a place in Irish showbiz history when my song, 'What's Another Year', sung by Johny Logan, won the Eurovision Song Contest in The Hague, Holland. The song soared to the No. 1 spot in eleven countries and sold a million and a half singles. Johnny Logan became a sex symbol and I became a national figure, which is a symbol without the sex. For someone who craved recognition, being a symbol suited me fine and the next five years was a feast for the ego of unimaginable proportions.

At this point I should have been home free. I was thirty-seven years old and this extraordinary piece of good fortune should have become the platform to eternal riches and a life of ease. Instead I was pretty reckless and, apart from dining well and enjoying my celebrity status, I didn't do much else of note, other than squander my royalties on champagne, dreams and expensive demos. Mind you, I still have some of the classiest demos in Ireland to prove it, but when it came to using my lucky break, it might have been easier to listen to wiser heads than mine.

The lean years were pretty lean and in 1986, desperation drove me back to television. I got as job as a reporter on a magazine show called 'Evening Extra'. That gave me back a high visual profile, mostly with the older generation. And then in 1988, I was lucky enough to be chosen to host 'Nighthawks'. The show became cult viewing and the rollercoaster was now heading up the hill again. 'Nighthawks' made me cool, and at forty-five I needed all the chill factor I could get. The show lasted four glorious years.

I picked up an older audience again when I presented a country music show, 'Music City USA'. That was followed by another left-field chatshow, 'The Birthday Show', which lasted for two seasons. But I could slowly feel myself starting to drown in a sea of antipathy within RTÉ and, though I was given one more stab with a nostalgia show, after one series the powers-that-be showed me the door. I was told that my style was 'old-fashioned'. Imagine – I went from being a cult to a similar-sounding four-letter word, all in the space of eight years.

Luckily, in 1991 I had branched out into becoming a producer/director on a series of documentaries, first with Declan Farrell and later with my brilliant colleague, Marion Cullen. For the past fifteen years I have been privileged to produce and/or direct documentaries about Roy Rogers, Tammy Wynette, Phil Lynott, New York cop Chris Byrne, Billie Barry, Mosney Holiday Camp, Ronan Tynan and the Hawk's Well Theatre.

Today I am still a film-maker, writer, photographer, journalist and songwriter. For the past twelve years, I have been happy to be in the background, working quietly. Sometimes I find it hard to believe that the shameless exhibitionist I once was could welcome back anonymity so readily. The truth is I draw great comfort from being able to melt back into the crowd and I am more than happy to leave fame and the limelight to the mayfly celebrities of this modern era.

I enjoyed my time in the sun, but here's the really ironic bit and it will give you a laugh. Despite having dabbled in so many different disciplines and convinced myself what a great guy I was and am, when I meet people, the opening question is never, 'What are *you* working on now?' or, 'How is *your* songwriting going?' or 'Where do you get your ideas?' No. The question they invariably ask is: 'WHAT'S JOHNNY LOGAN DOING NOW?'

Now that's what I call putting things in perspective.